Higher Education Policy Series 24

Assessing Quality in Further and Higher Education

Allan Ashworth and Roger C. Harvey

Jessica Kingsley Publishers
London and Bristol, Pennsylvania

The views expressed by the authors are their own. They do not necessarily represent those of any present or previous employers.

First published in the United Kingdom in 1994 by
Jessica Kingsley Publishers Ltd
116 Pentonville Road
London N1 9JB, England
 and
1900 Frost Road, Suite 101
Bristol, PA 19007, U S A

Copyright © 1994 Allan Ashworth and Roger C. Harvey
Foreword copyright © 1994 Professor Ken Goulding

British Library Cataloguing in Publication Data
Ashworth, A.
Quality in Further and Higher Education
– (Higher Education Policy Series
Vol.24)
I. Title II. Harvey, R. III. Series
378.1

ISBN 1 85302 539 9

Printed and Bound in Great Britain by
Biddles Ltd, Guildford and King's Lynn

Assessing Quality in Further and Higher Education

of related interest

The Use of Performance Indicators in Higher Education
A Critical Analysis of Developing Practice, 2nd Edition
Martin Cave, Stephen Hanney and Maurice Kogan
ISBN 1 85302 518 6
Higher Education Policy Series 3

Self-Regulation in Higher Education
A Multi-National Perspective on Collaborative Systems
  of Quality Assurance and Control
H.R. Kells
ISBN 1 85302 528 3
Higher Education Policy Series 15

Evaluating Higher Education
Edited by Maurice Kogan
ISBN 1 85302 510 0
Higher Education Policy Series 6

Dimensions of Evaluation in Higher Education
Report of the IHME Study Group on Evaluation
  in Higher Education
Urban Dahllöff, John Harris, Michael Shattock,
  André Staropoli and Roeland in't Veld
ISBN 1 85302 526 7
Higher Education Policy Series 13

Are Professors Professional?
The Organisations of University Examinations
David Warren Piper
ISBN 1 85302 540 2
Higher Education Policy Series 25

Contents

List of Tables

List of Figures

---

* grid charts

Foreword

Institutions of Higher and Further Education (HFE) are currently embarked upon a period of considerable change. It can be argued that there is nothing new in this: HFE has been subject to change almost constantly over a considerable period of time. Many 'buzz-words' associated with change have come and gone over the last fifteen to twenty years. Often they arose from the work of the Council for National Academic Awards (CNAA) and the Further Education Unit (FEU) working respectively with the rapidly evolving Polytechnics and the more forward looking Further Education Colleges.

But the current period of change is, arguably, unprecedented. Moreover, it is clear that some of the current buzz-words will be around for some time. One of these is Quality. Discussion of quality standards, quality indicators, quality audit and quality assessment (teaching and research) abound in the staff rooms, common rooms and meeting rooms of all FHE institutions.

Much of the discussion is animated with increasing concern that external (the Higher and Further Funding Councils and the Higher Education Quality Council) and internal systems of quality assurance, enhancement and assessment are demanding too much of FHE institutions – ironically to the long-term detriment of quality. There has been much recent posturing on this issue by the Committee of Vice-Chancellors and Principals (CVCP) but Government (and the Funding Councils?) remain adamant that quality must be assessed and audited.

The three Higher Education Funding Councils (England, Scotland and Wales) have separate systems of Quality Assessment based on pilot schemes which, in general, have not cultivated a great deal of the support or confidence from the Universities or Institutions of Higher Education. The Further Education Funding Council in England is introducing its system of quality assessment based upon an inspectorate.

What are the key issues of quality assessment and audit? How are they best undertaken? What is the role of self-assessment? Can and will institutions be judged 'in accordance with their missions' or will we see mission drift? What is the relationship between quality and students in FHE? These and many other questions are posed in this book, written by two experienced practitioners in a thought provoking way. The outcome represents an important and authoritative contribution to the, so called, Quality Debate.

Professor Ken Goulding
Deputy Vice Chancellor (Academic)
Middlesex University

Preface

... the Government attaches great importance to systems which will ensure the quality of education and training in the colleges.

Education and Training for the 21st Century

Quality, according to the dictionary, is: 'a degree of excellence but of a relative nature'. It is sometimes described in terms of excellence – that is, the highest quality – or in terms of fitness for purpose. However, a product that conforms consistently to an appropriate pre-defined specification or standard can be said to be a quality product. Failure consistently to meet specification would cast doubts on the product's quality. Setting, and meeting, a higher grade specification would also result in a quality product, but of better quality than that of the former.

Thus, quality is set by an educational institution within its own specification, or mission statement. Having decided on this specification, the mechanisms and procedures must be in place to meet it consistently. If they are not, and the college falls short of its pre-defined standards, then it cannot be said to be a quality institution and must work to a lower grade specification.

The maintenance of the appropriate level of quality within an educational institution is a major issue which has only recently received the attention it deserves. Senior management teams within colleges have often been perplexed when faced with an array of different management tools purporting to relate to the maintenance of quality and, sometimes, have lost sight of the two main objectives. These are:

- to maintain the quality of the students' experience
- to maintain the standards achieved by the students.

In short, whatever organisational arrangements and procedures are introduced into colleges which are geared to maintain and improve, for example, managerial performance, administrative systems or staff motivation, the acid test is the influence of these changes on the quality of the students' experience and the standards achieved by them. Have these aspects of the college's work benefited? Maintaining, or achieving improvements in quality whilst attempting to meet the continuing requirement of 'doing more with less' lays down challenges for senior management teams. Nonetheless, these objectives are not mutually exclusive; rather, they are closely linked.

In a climate in which funding bodies and assessors expect colleges to 'know themselves' by means of self assessment, this handbook is designed to give participants in further and higher education an analysis of precepts governing the maintenance and improvement of quality. Many of the figures and tables are representative of typical field data. Where appropriate, the work of others is acknowledged.

Allan Ashworth
Roger C. Harvey
May 1993

Student Participation in Further and Higher Education

There has been a considerable expansion in student enrolments in further and higher education, not only in the United Kingdom but throughout Europe, the rest of the western world and the developing nations. This expansion is occurring at a time of falling demographic trends amongst the industrialised nations and a recession that has had a greater impact upon society than the recession of the 1930s. Enrolments in higher education (HE), for example, increased from 534,300 (377,700 full-time) in 1980 to 740,000 (525,600 full-time) by 1990. They are projected to exceed one million by the year 2000. In further education (FE), the Government has planned that, from 1993, enrolments will increase by 8 per cent per year for each of the next three years. The increased participation levels have required governments to reorganise the education system; increase the number of student places; redesignate some colleges and increase funding – but only at the margins of resource. The increased participation rates have been encouraged by improved student performances at GCSE and A-levels. For example, at GCSE, 24 per cent gained five passes at C grade and above in 1979/80 compared with 35 per cent in 1989/90. In 1979/80 only 8.6 per cent of the age group obtained three or more A-levels (49.5% of those who sat). In 1989/90 these figures had increased to 10.8 per cent and 56.5 per cent respectively. There was also a wider acceptance of vocational qualifications as a means of entry into HE, particularly amongst the former polytechnics, and those which offered vocationally orientated programmes of study. The number of students on Business and Technology Education Council (BTEC) national diploma programmes in further education increased from 51,000 (17,700 full-time) to 63,000 (41,500 full-time). Coupled with these increases and the concomitant expectations amongst school leavers has been the additional demands made by more mature students to improve their own education and qualifications at different levels in both further and higher education.

The numbers of 18-year-olds in the population reached its peak in 1984 with almost one million individuals. This is projected to decline to a trough in 1995 of about 650,000. Not all of these enter further or higher education, but the decline in numbers is less pronounced in those social classes which have traditionally under-taken education beyond that of compulsory schooling. In addition, a greater number of young people are choosing to continue in part-time or full-time education beyond the normal school leaving age. Post compulsory participation rates amongst 16-year-old school leavers increased from 42 per cent (28% school, 14% further education) in 1979 to 53 per cent (35% school, 18% FE) by 1989. A further 18 per cent of 16-year-olds were studying on a part-time basis in further education. These figures, whilst encouraging for Britain, compare poorly with the rest of Europe (e.g. Germany 71 per cent, France 82 per cent, Italy 70 per cent). The full-time participation rates for 17-year-olds increased from 36 per cent (27% school, 9% FE) to 53 per cent (38% school, 15% FE) over the same period.

A brief summary of the changes in the student population, observed since 1980, and trends that can be expected to continue into the early part of the next century are as follows:

- increases in both full-time and part-time student numbers
- increase in the numbers of mature students
- increases in students with non standard entry qualifications
- decline in overseas students due to an increasing self sufficiency in developing countries
- little increase in students from eastern Europe (possibly due to language barriers)
- increases in the numbers of post graduate students
- improvement in student performance at GCSE and A-levels
- increase in the number of students with vocational qualifications
- increase in student age cohort participation rates
- reduction in the numbers of applicants to places on programmes of study, due to a wide expansion of the latter
- whilst student expectations and achievements will continue to increase, employment opportunities are unlikely to meet these expectations.

The above changes in the number and ability ranges of students has had an impact upon the wide range of student services that are provided by colleges. The widening of entry qualifications has created a need to provide a more carefully structured arrangement of support services, all of which can have an effect upon the quality of the provision that is being offered. The challenge facing the educational system during the next decade is to maintain quality, whilst student numbers increase, at a reduced unit cost. Failure to meet this challenge effectively will result in a real reduction in output standards due to adjustments at the staff–student interface.

Chapter 1

Performance Indicators and Quality Grade Descriptors

> When you can measure what you are speaking of and express
> it in numbers you know that on which you are discoursing. But
> when you cannot measure it and express it in numbers your
> knowledge is of a very meagre and unsatisfactory kind.
>
> *Lord Kelvin*

The Education Industry: The Functions of Further and Higher Education Institutions

A college is a complex mechanism that is responsible for transforming a variety of inputs for example, students' time, teachers' time, consumable materials, equipment and buildings, into knowledge products usually in the forms of qualified people and intellectual property. The latter is the research component of knowledge. These products, in their turn, generate goods and services for society. The transformation is highly value added, although the means by which the mechanism carries out the transformation process is often obscure. The way in which people learn and develop ideas is closely individualistic and not easily understood. It is based largely on human interactions and relationships. The means used for measuring and manipulating aspects of the transformation have proved, historically, taxing and interference in the teaching traditions has caused resentment. In particular, the measurement of quality is an emotive issue.

Nonetheless, as much of human endeavour is subject to demands for efficiency improvement (i.e., 'doing more with less'), it is not unreasonable that educational activities have also been subjected to close inspection with the aim of improving efficiency while maintaining quality. This can be achieved, in part, by getting things right first time, which is a hallmark of good quality. Measures, or indicators, can be recorded at different points in the transformation process, most obviously at input and output, with a variety of different measurements included for the sub-processes. The development of these approaches has led to cost-benefit and cost-effective analyses and the emergence of management statistics and performance indicators. The techniques can be complicated and, to an extent, undermined by the difficulties in legitimately allocating costs within the transformation; the sensitivity of the outcomes to the initial assumptions is referred to in the following sections.

Cost-Benefit Analysis

This technique has been used to establish the returns to investment in education. In other words, if education is a form of capital, what is the rate of return to it and how does it compare with other forms of investment? Is it subject to diminishing returns? This analysis, based on the discounted value of the investments in earnings associated with education compared with the costs of that education, has been carried out for individual students and economies as a whole (Psacharopoulis 1985). Clearly, it is not an easy analysis to carry out as both costs and benefits can be difficult to disaggregate. Yet more difficult to establish are the corresponding analyses for the research components of knowledge, although some first stage analyses have been undertaken for individual products (Institution of Civil Engineers 1988).

Calculation of the returns made for a number of countries indicate that:

- the rate of return declines with the level of education
- the profitability of investment in women's education is greater than in that of men
- in general, diminishing returns have not followed an expansion in higher education
- there is a considerable margin for reducing the public subsidisation of higher education.

Cost-Effective Analysis

A cost-effective analysis appears to be relatively straightforward, but this is not always the case. If the analysis is conducted on the basis of input and output costs for different areas of activity within a college, the allocations of the overhead in the costs presents difficulties. The overhead includes costs for which the following are examples:

- learning resources such as libraries and computer suites
- accommodation
- laboratory equipment
- management services.

Should the programme of study overhead be allocated simply on a pro-rata basis to the college overhead, be directly related to teaching costs or be allocated in some other manner? Analyses can show the same programme of study to be either cost-effective or in deficit depending on the overhead assumption adopted. As with the cost-benefit analysis, there is an indication as to whether or not the activity under consideration should be undertaken, however tenuous.

Alternatively, inputs can be cost related and the outputs presented in some other units; for example, proportion of students achieving the qualification. This is a convenient way in which comparisons of courses can be made, either within or across disciplines. The outputs can often be calculated quickly and easily on a disaggregated basis. Not only can outputs be compared in this way, but the procedure is also applicable to inputs and other aspects of the transformation process. Measures of this kind are known as performance indicators.

Performance Indicators

Performance indicators are statistics, ratios and other quantitative information which indicate the way in which a programme of study or a college is operating. The performance indicators used should relate to the mission statement of the college and, over a period of time, may confirm, or otherwise, whether the college is making progress in meeting the objectives set out in the mission statement. Just as performance indicators can be used to make comparisons between colleges, they can be used to make comparisons between parts of colleges, but they should be used with great care. Performance indicators should be used not as an end in themselves to draw definitive conclusions, but to trigger areas of concern and provide a catalyst for further investigation. If performance indicators are not used to facilitate decision making and day-to-day management, they are likely to fall into disrepute and be disregarded.

Hence, the main features of performance indicators in supporting the management process may be summarised as follows:

- relevant to the mission statement of the institution

- assist in the monitoring and evaluation of the institution's activities

- provide data by which to make judgements on resource allocations

- assist in forward planning and decision making

- acceptance by, and motivation of, staff.

Many sets of performance indicators have been devised. For example, the University Management Statistics and Performance Indicators, 1990 (Appendix 1) seem comprehensive but are unimpressive as a management tool. In comparison, the Polytechnics and Colleges Funding Council's (PCFC) sets of performance indicators (Appendix 2) have proved more relevant and are more easily handled. Nonetheless, few, if any, performance indicators have yet received general acceptance in the academic world.

In order to develop a first stage set of performance indicators which describe a college's activity, it is instructive to consider some of the factors to be taken into account in evaluating quality, or fitness for purpose (Heythrop Park Report, 1989).

Measurement of Quality

Quality in the transformation of the inputs is taken to be concerned with the factors involved in the process and their fitness for purpose. For example:

- staffing

- accommodation

- equipment

- teaching and learning
- standards achieved
- management and quality control.

Quality is assessed within the frame of reference imposed by the programmes of study and, in some cases, for example teaching and learning, judgements can be more elusive than in other cases. However, quality judgements about the transformation factors are inextricably interrelated and correlation coefficients are presented in Appendix 3.

Staffing

The teaching staff is a college's most important resource. A good staff establishment would comprise an appropriately sized group of well qualified and experienced individuals with a range of academic and professional qualifications matched to the programme of study portfolio. The experience of the staff would include academic and vocational/professional experience and these industrial/professional links would serve to enrich the curriculum. Further enhancement would be expected by research and consultancy work relevant to the teaching programmes. Staff development plays an essential role in ensuring the up-to-dateness and relevance of staff expertise. Part-time and visiting staff also provide a measure of breadth and expertise. To ensure the completeness of the staff team and to enable it to undertake its teaching role effectively, it is essential to have an appropriate level and deployment of non-teaching support, both technicians and administrative staff.

In short, the key features relating to quality are:
- size, qualifications and match of staff team to curricula; this includes part-time staff
- experience, both academic and external/professional
- staff development.

Accommodation

The programmes of study need to have the benefit of an adequate amount of teaching accommodation, both general and specialist, which is suitable in type and location. The rooms must be properly furnished with a range of services to offer the teachers the opportunity to use a variety of teaching strategies and approaches in an environment which is clean, comfortable and free from extraneous noise.

The accommodation must be safe and easily accessible for all students during its use throughout the whole of the college day. Room deployment which gives a close match between rooms, teaching activities and group sizes is an indicator of effective management. Where required, technical and other support staff are necessary to allow the effectiveness and efficient use of the facilities. The accommodation is necessarily a learning environment which provides stimulation through reference materials and artefacts relevant to teaching programmes.

Summarising, the key features relating to quality are:

- the amount, type and location of the accommodation
- furnishings, services and physical environment
- access and safety
- well managed deployment of clean, well maintained accommodation
- availability of support staff
- effective and stimulating learning environment.

Equipment

Courses which need the use of specialist equipment to help to teach the students in an appropriate manner depend upon that equipment being fit for the purpose. For example, if the equipment available for practical work does not match the programme specialisms or student numbers are too large, then it is unsuitable in range and adequacy. Even if the available equipment meets the specified criteria, students may still not benefit if it is ineffectively managed, with failure to properly deploy or maintain it, thus reducing student access and use. Proper maintenance frequently demands the support of a suitable number of trained technicians. Departments need to have programmes for the planned replacement of equipment which is becoming dated and approaching obsolescence. Even before this stage is reached, it may be too expensive to maintain properly, causing the available budget to be unhelpfully skewed. Modern state-of-the-art equipment can be extremely expensive and it may not be possible to provide equipment to contemporary industrial standards. Under the circumstances, it can be possible to arrange visits to industrial organisations to allow students to gain an insight into up-to-date practice.

The main aspects necessary to ensure an appropriate student experience in courses with an element of practical work are that:

- the amount and range of equipment are appropriate
- the equipment is effectively deployed, maintained and, when necessary, replaced by more appropriate equipment
- students have proper access to the equipment which is effectively utilised.

Teaching and learning

In forming judgements about teaching and learning, it is not just the individual sessions that are judged but also the way in which the individual sessions contribute to the totality of the teaching programme. In particular, several factors are considered:

- the framework in which the teaching session takes place
- the context of the teaching session
- what happens during the teaching session
- the outcomes from the teaching session.

It is important that the teaching programme is well organised to form a coherent programme of study with both teaching staff and students in full understanding of the objectives of the programme and each element of the programme. Programme guides are essential. To achieve the objectives it is often necessary to utilise the learning resources and it should be expected that laboratories, workshops, studios, library and other learning materials can be accessed to support teaching and facilitate learning.

Within the teaching session itself, judgements must be made regarding the teaching content and the way in which the teacher presents the session. Is it paced appropriately with the teaching material pitched in such a way that the students are challenged? Is the role of the teacher such that, by active or passive techniques, learning is facilitated; or does the teaching strategy obscure learning? As students learn in different ways, there is advantage in devising a variety of teaching techniques to match the different learning needs. Often students become closely involved; they interact with the teachers and develop as reproductive or under-standing learners. What is the expectation of the teacher?

As learning takes place both within and outwith the classroom, judgements must be made about the tasks which students are set; are they of an appropriate standard and do they offer progressive stages in terms of degrees of difficulty? The assessment of these tasks is an important consideration as the way in which this is done informs the students of their progress and must be appropriate in properly measuring the skills and understandings of the students. The assessment techniques may advantageously be designed as learning sessions for the students. In this way, an understanding of the students' performance, and how this may be enhanced, is acquired by the students.

The most nebulous aspect of teaching and learning is the amount of learning that takes place. This can be when a permanent change in an individual's response is noted which is progressive in terms of successfully completing their programme of studies. In summary, judgements on quality are made taking into account the following factors:

- the input of the teachers

- the response of the students

across the individual teaching sessions and the teaching pro-gramme in its entirety by reference to the many contributing factors outlined above.

Standards achieved

Whether or not the quality of learning can easily be judged in the teaching sessions, there is no doubt that it can be made more evident by examining the quality of work in the students' course-work and written examinations. Of prime importance are the standards achieved, the manner in which the standards are main-tained and how the level of the students' performance is reflected in the overall examination classifications. Not only is it essential to have a mechanism in place which is rigorous in the way in which it arrives at these classifications, but the reputation and integrity of the external examiners and moderators is an integral part of the system. The accurate monitoring of progression and decisions taken if the withdrawal and failure rates are high are an indication of how the programme team is operating and the attitude of the institution to student progress. Finally, the progression of students to employment, having completed their programme of study, reflects the value and reputation of the qualification obtained.

The judgements made on standards are reflected in the following factors:

- the mechanisms which ensure the appropriate maintenance of standards
- the achievements of the students
- the employment destinations of the students.

Management and quality control

One of the major responsibilities of management is to ensure that an appropriate mechanism operates within the institution to maintain an effective level of quality control. This impacts on decisions relating to economic realities as well as educational ideals and involves a close appreciation of the factors outlined below the subheadings above. These verbal descriptions can often be categorised more concisely by use of the following quality grade descriptors 1 to 5:

1. Very good with many good characteristics.
2. Good, good characteristics and no major shortcomings.
3. Sound but undistinguished, or good characteristics balanced by shortcomings.
4. Some shortcomings in important areas.
5. Many shortcomings, generally poor.

Thus, a quality assessment is made of an activity or facility by inspecting the mix of the desirable (i.e., good), and undesirable (i.e., causing shortcomings) characteristics present. Judgement is used to decide whether or not, for example, the activities with some good characteristics are in fact good. Often this is the case if there are no major shortcomings. A similar procedure is used when judging whether or not an activity is unsatisfactory, that is, showing some shortcomings in important areas. Necessarily, the activity or facility characteristics need definitions to initiate the quality assessment process and subsequent judgement essential to designate a valid grade descriptor. These aspects form the central theme of the following chapters.

Just as the procedure for the development of a grade descriptor can be used for individual activities and facilities, and so forth, it can also be applied to sets of activities and facilities. This process of successive integrations can be used as widely as required; for example, to judge the overall quality of a college's accommodation, or the overall quality of a sample of teaching sessions of a department or faculty.

Quality control is a term normally used to describe the operational techniques or systematic procedures which are carried out to check that the products conform to specification. Statistical information and performance indicators are part of the system. Quality assurance refers to the checks made to ensure that the control procedures are followed.

The following are general principles concerned with quality systems in further and higher education:

- a recognition of fitness for purpose based upon agreed objectives and standards
- the need to set quality issues with the institution's own strategic plans or mission statement
- a recognition that quality must be planned and managed
- all aspects need to be focused upon since quality is only as strong as the weakest link
- the need for some form of continuous monitoring system
- an acknowledgement of the merits of the different quality control and assurance systems which are available
- an emphasis towards quality enhancement
- a recognition of the importance of the committed programme team
- the need for accountability to the institution's customers, such as students and employers
- a concern for value for money
- a recognition that quality and the absence of it both have economic consequences.

There are several management models used to exercise quality assurance and control which were designed outside the educational context but, nonetheless, have been applied to education. Two of these are BS 5750 and total quality management (TQM).

BS 5750

This general purpose standard, to which a quality management system can be required to conform, was initially designed for the mass production manufacturing/engineering industry in which it is essential to adhere to a specified technical standard. Each step of the process is controlled by means of procedures manuals which can be time consuming in their preparation and operation. Guidelines have been finalised for converting the BS 5750 clauses to the needs of education and training. The source of difficulty in the conversion process has been the product definition under BS 5750. Rather than being the student, who is the customer, the product is, for example, the learning process, student learning or student entitlement. Clearly, it is more difficult to achieve product consistency with an educational product than with an engineering product. This is a common difficulty with service industries where product quality depends on interactions between customer and supplier.

The BS 5750 system tends to be bureaucratic, emphasising a top-down procedure with the assumption that procedures are unlikely to change in the shorter term. The BS 5750 registration mark confirms that the system itself conforms to the required standard rather than that the output from the system meets a required specification. Nonetheless, properly implemented, the BS 5750 system has proved beneficial in many companies establishing a discipline in the operation of quality producing procedures. It can also be a potentially powerful marketing tool. Colleges may find that businesses with which they deal as training providers may require registration with BS 5750 as they do with other suppliers. If required, the BS 5750 can be applied, in part, to the college activities, for example, services as a sub-contractor. In summary, the main features of BS 5750 are:

- a well documented but somewhat bureaucratic system
- well defined procedures and processes
- clearly defined standards for the quality system
- product consistency may be difficult to achieve
- can be applied to only one area of the college's activities
- is audited by a third party.

Total Quality Management (TQM)

TQM is a system that seeks to realign the mission, culture and working practices of an organisation by means of pursuing continued quality improvement. This process, which is founded on the individual attitude and effort in quality improvement, emphasises a commitment to satisfy the needs of the customer both inside and outside an organisation. In contrast to the BS 5750, TQM does not set out to meet a pre-defined quality goal but, rather, seeks continually to improve quality by a process of research, evaluation and feedback. Once areas capable of improvement can be defined, resources can be applied to effect an improvement. TQM can be introduced only gradually and lacks the specificity of BS 5750 in the way in which the culture change can be introduced. Indeed, an initial adoption and implementation of BS 5750 may be a first step towards the advancement of TQM. Once TQM is adopted, an organisation is on a path of continuous quality improvement by challenging current practices and performance with a view to improvement.

The main features of TQM are:

- a college wide commitment to quality
- a focus on satisfying customers' needs
- a commitment to continuous quality improvement
- all staff responsible for achieving quality outcomes.

A sub-set of TQM is known as Strategic Quality Management (SQM). SQM focuses close attention on the needs of the learner and how the quality of the learning experience can be assured. The learners' needs relate to pre-entry, entry, on programme and exit. Within this framework the key characteristics relating to quality are identified and standards set within the available resource levels. Quality control is the responsibility of the programme team; quality assurance is overseen by the middle managers with the SQM monitored by the senior management. This is a model which has found favour in many colleges but, like TQM, lacks third party accreditation.

Performance Indicators Describing Provision, Process and Progress (outcomes)

Based on the description of the areas of activity, some first-stage groups of performance indicators are shown in Table 1.1. These relate to provision (or inputs), process and progress (or outputs). Although most of these performance indicators are background indicators to quality, a few are considered as quality indicators.

Table 1.1: Groups of performance indicators

First ideas on the performance indicators to be used; these are global performance indicators as opposed to local performance indicators; disaggregation is necessary.

1. Provision

Area per FTE student: A

Staffing budget/total expenditure: STE

Buildings expenditure/ total expenditure (or buildings expenditure/per full-time equivalent (FTE) student): BTE

Capital expenditure/total expenditure (or capital expenditure/per FTE student): CTE

Staff development (SD) budget/total expenditure: SDTE

Properties of catchment area: z

Unit costs: UC

Marketing expenditure/total expenditure: MTE

Local performance indicators: Students enrolled/target enrolment; library provision; computing provision and disaggregation generally.

2. Process

Student/staff ratio: SSR

Academic staff/support staff ratio: AS

Average student hours: ASH

Average lecturer hours: ALH

Average class size: ACS

% attendance: %A

Quality of teaching and learning as compared to national teaching and learning: QTL

Space utilisation: SU

Consumables expenditure/total expenditure (or consumables
   expenditure/per FTE student): COTE
Part-time staff hours/full-time staff hours: PF

Local performance indicators: quality of staff and disaggregation generally

3. *Progress (or outcomes)*
   * Examination results (success rate): ExR
   * Staying on ratio: SO
   Progression to FHE/postgraduate studies: PFHE
   Employment record: ER
   * Added value: AV
   Income/total expenditure: ITE
   Research output: RO

Local performance indicators: Moderators reports and disaggregation generally, e.g. research income, etc.

   * designated as a quality indicator

A distinction has been made between global performance indicators as a national measurement of performance and local performance indicators. Typical sets of data are shown in Table 1.2 which indicate the performance indicators as a national average for further and higher education. Also shown are first stage upper and lower bound performance indicators. The data for a typical college are shown in graphical form in Figure 1.1. These indicate that the performance of a typical college can be quickly appreciated when set against the national performance.

It should be emphasised that these data sets do not constitute a judgement, but indicate areas that could be more closely examined. For example, although the college shown in Figure 1.1 performs at near national average in many respects, some buildings might be run down; income is low and should be investigated; consumables are a little low.

The following sections examine briefly a number of performance indicators and indicate techniques for their comparison.

Table 1.2: Sets of performance indicators for further education and higher education (in brackets)

PI	Lower bound	National average	Upper bound
A	5.0 (8.5)sq.m.	8.5 (11.5)sq.m.	13.0 (16.5)sq.m.
STE	71 (73)%	77 (75)%	85 (81)%
BTE	7.9 (10.6)%	9.4 (10.8)%	10.9 (11.6)%
CTE	0 (na)%	1.0 (na)%	1.5 (na)%
SDTE	0.1 (0.5)%	1.5 (1.5)%	2.0 (2.5)%
UC	£1900 (3400)	£2250 (3650)	£2820 (4000)
MTE	0.7 (na)%	1.0 (na)%	2.0 (na)%
SSR	10.5 (9.0)	11.8 (12.3)	14.0 (18.0)
AS	1.5 (1.5)	4.0 (3.0)	5.0 (5.0)
ASH	20.0 (8.0)	23.1 (18.7)	24.7 (26.0)
ALH	17.0 (6.0)	18.4 (16.1)	20.2 (18.0)
ACS	10.8 (12.2)	14.7 (14.3)	20.0 (25.0)
%A	65 (60)%	80 (80)%	90 (90)%
QTL	0.24 (0.30)	0.30 (0.48)	0.62 (0.90)
SU	0.40 (0.40)	0.50 (0.49)	0.60 (0.65)
COTE	7.0 (na)%	7.9 (na)%	9.6 (na)%
PF	17 (na)%	25 (na)%	40 (na)%
ExR	0.60 (0.76)	0.70 (0.90)	0.80 (0.98)
SO	0.39 (0.80)	0.40 (0.90)	0.42 (0.95)
PFHE	0.10 (0.05)	0.15 (0.10)	0.39 (0.15)
ER	0.50 (0.74)	0.76 (0.92)	0.81 (0.97)
AV	na (na)	na (na)	na (na)
ITE	14 (na)%	25 (na)%	32 (na)%
RO	– (na)	– (na)	– (na)

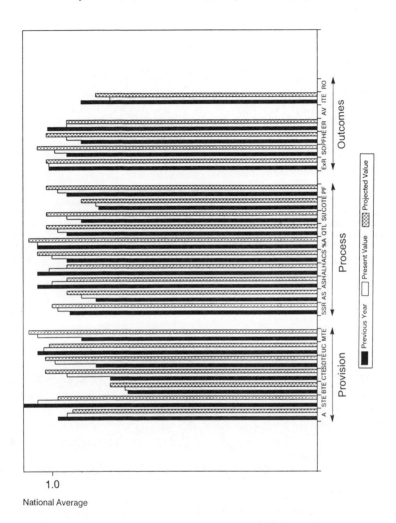

Figure 1.1: Performance indicators for a typical college

Staffing budget/total expenditure: STE

In further education colleges the average staffing costs are 77 per cent of the total expenditure; on average, 60 per cent is spent on academic staffing and 17 per cent on support staffing. The proportion of the budget spent on staffing emphasises the fact that education is a people-centred industry. Colleges which spend, for example, over 80 per cent of total expenditure on staffing find it more difficult to provide adequate learning resources or maintain accommodation to good standards. High levels of spending on staffing can indicate:

- other areas are under resourced, for example, learning resources
- identified areas of staff expenditure may be excessive; for example, support staff
- student/staff ratios are low
- average class sizes are low
- curricula are overfull
- programmes of study are overtaught.

Part-time staff hours/full-time staff hours: PF

To reduce recurrent staffing costs, senior management teams have, in many cases, reduced the numbers of full-time teachers in favour of part-time teaching staff. Apart from colleges in which there is a large amount of adult education, the ratio of part-time to full-time hours is often about 1:4. Increasing part-time teaching numbers has the tendency to:

- put greater administrative burdens on a relatively small full-time team
- unless care is taken, diminish the quality of student support and experience
- fragment the teaching team and make it more difficult to achieve its objectives by way of a unified team curriculum delivery.

In some cases, the proportion of part-time hours has reduced and, although this has a number of advantages, disadvantages can include:

- the programme team tends to be 'locked into' a curriculum offer
- the breadth of industrial/commercial experience, often introduced by part-time staff, is not available to the students.

Added Value: AV

Added value is the contribution that a college makes to the development of its students. From the academic standpoint added value can be defined as the ratio of output profile points to input profile points calculated on a group basis with allowance for withdrawal and maturity; the calculation is simply performed for the students' cohorts. It compares students' performances within and across subject disciplines, although care needs to be exercised depending on the relationship between entry qualifications and the nature of the learning programme. Added value is an amalgam of entry qualifications, withdrawal rates, exit qualifications and, implicitly, the z-score for the catchment area; that is, the level of disadvantage and its influence on prior achievement, or significantly, motivation. Use of added value highlights a number of issues; for example:

- overall achievement by students in academic terms
- the influence of withdrawal
- the relative performance of different groups of students
- the exercise of discretion by boards of examiners.

An added value analysis is not merely a quantitative analysis. It is a management tool which assists in the identification of strengths and weaknesses by the interpretation of the issues raised by the added value analysis.

Regression Analysis

In making comparisons between the outputs of different academic areas, the relative sizes of departments, sections or units is a factor worthy of consideration. This may apply to research outputs, for example, in which it may be necessary to adjust outputs per member of staff depending on the size of the section in which they work. This can be done using regression analysis which is a mathematical model which best describes the data collected. In situations in which the relationship between the variables is not explicit, a regression analysis provides a statistical technique to quantify this relationship.

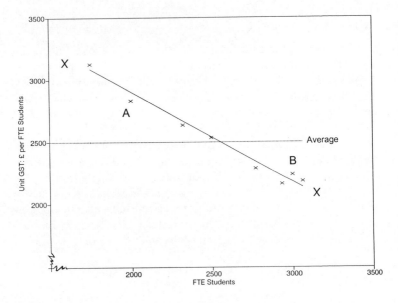

Figure 1.2: Regression analysis for unit cost data

Figure 1.2 shows the unit cost data for a number of further education colleges of different sizes. The average level of unit cost for all colleges is shown by the horizontal line in Figure 1.2. The data suggest that the larger colleges are more efficient in their use of resources and, using statistical regression analysis, this is shown to be the case, line xx.

The following conclusions may be drawn:

- large colleges are more efficient

- college B is above average efficiency and college A is below average efficiency
- adjusted data based on size shows that college A is performing better than might be expected whilst college B is performing worse than might be expected.

Regression analysis allows an evaluation to take place by comparing the actual outputs with the expected outputs for a given level of outputs. In this sense, it is a refined and perceptive technique.

References

HMI Invitation Conference (1989) 'In pursuit of quality: an HMI view', *Quality in Higher Education. Heythrop Park Proceedings.* June, pp.3–15.

Psacharopoulis, G. (1985) 'Returns to education; a further international update and implications. *Journal of Human Relations,* 4, 583–604.

The Institution of Civil Engineers (1988) *Research funding in the construction industry.* ICE September pp.27–35.

Further Reading

Cave, M., Hanney, S. and Kogan, M. (1991) *The Use of Performance Indicators in Higher Education* 2nd edition. London: Jessica Kingsley Publishers.

Combe Lodge Report (1987) *Performance Indicators: Theory and Practice.* Volume 20, No.1. The Further Education Staff College.

CNAA (1990) Performance indicators and quality assurance. Information. Services discussion.

HMI Report (1990) *Performance Indicators in Higher Education.* London: Department of Education and Science.

Johnes, J. and Taylor, J. (1990) *Performance Indicators in Higher Education.* The Society for Research into Higher Education and Open University Press.

Portsmouth Polytechnic (1989) *Performance Indicators and Quality Control in Higher Education.* Conference held at Institute of Education, University of London.

Scottish Education Department (1990) *Measuring Up: Performance Indicators in Further Education. Report by HMI of Schools.* London: HMSO.

Chapter 2

Organisation and Resources

...enjoy to the full the resources that are within thy reach.

Pythian Odes

Organisation Structures

Educational institutions are a combination of different components. These include staff, students and programmes of study, and buildings and equipment that can be utilised in the educational process. The arrangement of programmes varies in the different sorts of college and is partially related to tradition, expediency, size and the nature of the activities being undertaken. Most colleges are organised on a departmental basis where similar discipline programmes, students and the majority of associated teachers are managed in a single unit. These units or departments vary in size, the smallest having about ten staff and the larger over seventy. The majority of teachers and students in this arrangement are able to easily identify with each other, and the department provides a clear focus for visitors and employers. In the smaller colleges, the arrangement is sometimes different, due largely to the size of the homogeneous groups. A matrix structure is more common. In this case the programmes of study are managed separately from the teachers; these then service the respective courses on a college-wide basis.

Irrespective of the arrangement, management is the process of ensuring that the aims and objectives that have been set by the college are met and the targets achieved. These include:

- identifying the items to be monitored
- estimating values for these variables
- implementing the process

- monitoring the system including collecting the relevant data and information
- feeding back the results and deciding what action needs to be taken
- using the information for setting revised targets for the future.

In the measurement of this performance three factors are considered:

- **effectiveness** what has been achieved through the above process, and have targets been met?
- **efficiency** what resources were necessary in achieving these objectives?
- **economy** could the process have been managed in a more cost effective way.

Feedback

Figure 2.1 shows that quality enhancement and improvement is a loop system that must be closed.

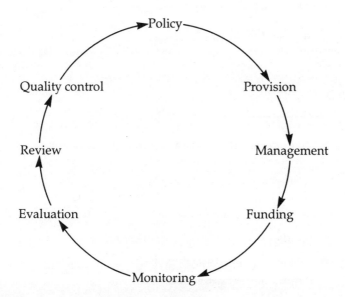

Figure 2.1: Closing the loop on quality

Mission statements

Colleges are measured against the objectives which management have set out in their published statement of purpose or mission statement, and how well these objectives are achieved in practice. Typically this will identify

- the college's aspirations
- its client groups
- the services that are offered
- the opportunities which are available
- the expectations in terms of quality.

Individual departments and all members of staff need to have a working knowledge of the mission statement, be able to identify it in their programme of study documents, and to demonstrate how programmes own it. In addition to the broad mission of a college there is also a set of aims, objectives and milestones for their achievement. The frequency of the review of the mission statement, who contributes and determines it, and the priorities within it also need to be examined. In addition to the mission statement most colleges set out a more detailed range of aims and objectives identifying goals that are expected to be achieved within specified time periods.

Using the quality grade descriptors given in Chapter 1, the following characteristics are used to judge the quality of the management of the college:

1. Very good, i.e., showing many of the following characteristics:

- strategic planning at college, faculty and departmental levels
- planning is both a combination of management and departmental views
- rolling programmes of objectives
- all staff are aware of plans
- forecasts are realistic and based upon industrial and social trends
- college structure meets needs
- senior managers are effective leaders
- all staff are well deployed

- leadership is proactive
- high level of morale
- staff relationships are generally very good
- structure provides for clear accountability at all levels
- programme teams meet at regular intervals
- quality control systems have a high priority throughout the college
- extensive use is made of performance indicators
- college has clear and open lines of communication.

2. Good, i.e., showing some of the good characteristics listed in (1) above with no major shortcomings.

3. Satisfactory, i.e., sound but undistinguished, or good characteristics balanced by shortcomings:

- strategic plans prepared by senior managers
- planning includes aspects of departmental expectations
- programme of future objectives
- staff can be informed of future activities
- forecasts rely upon local and general knowledge only
- college structure is appropriate for present arrangements
- senior managers are appropriate to the needs of the college
- staff are generally deployed effectively in the college
- leadership is aware of the needs of the college
- morale generally high amongst most staff
- relationships amongst most members of staff are satisfactory
- accountability is generally achieved at all levels
- calendar of programme team meetings'
- quality control is being achieved in many areas of activity
- performance data is used and recorded for major programme components
- lines of communication throughout the college are generally satisfactory.

Table 2.1: Management		
	Very Good: 1	*Good: 2*
Planning	Strategic planning at college, faculty and departmental levels. Planning is both a combination of management and departmental views. Rolling programme of objectives. All staff are aware of plans.	Strategic plans are largely the remit of senior managers. Planning uses departmental expectations as a basis. Rolling programme of objectives. Most staff are aware of plans.
Forecasting	Forecasts are realistic and based upon industrial and social trends.	Forecasts use a range of industrial and social trends.
Organising	The college structure fully meets its needs. Senior management are effective leaders. All staff are well deployed.	The college structure satisfies most academic units. Senior managers are good leaders. Most of the staff are well deployed.
Motivating	Leadership is proactive. There is a high level of morale. Staff relationships are generally very good.	Leadership is forward looking. Morale is good amongst most members of staff. Relationships generally are good.
Controlling	The structure provides for clear accountability at all levels.	Accountability is provided for at different levels in the college.
Co-ordinating	Programme teams meet at regular intervals. Quality control systems have a high priority throughout the college. Extensive use is made of performance indicators.	Programme teams meet at least once per term. Quality Control systems are implemented at the appropriate stages. Good use is made of performance indicators.
Communicating	The college has clear and open lines of communication.	Lines of communication are clear.

Table 2.1: Management		
Satisfactory: 3	*Unsatisfactory:* 4	*Poor:* 5
Strategic plans are prepared by senior managers. Planning includes aspects of departmental expectations. Programme of future objectives. Staff can be informed of future activities.	Departments have little input into overall objectives. Plans rely upon senior managers views of departmental expectations. Limited long term planning. Staff are generally not well informed about future plans.	No strategic plans. No consideration of departmental plans. Short term planning only. Staff are not informed of future developments.
Forecasts rely upon local and general knowledge only.	Forecasts are not based upon careful analysis of data.	Forecasts ignore any data or trends.
The college structure is appropriate for present arrangements. Senior managers are appropriate to the needs of the college. Staff are generally deployed effectively in the college.	The college structure uses an unsuitable model. Senior management are not effective. Staff are poorly deployed.	The college structure does not work effectively in practice. Senior management are not respected by the college staff. Staff are not properly deployed in their duties.
Leadership is aware of the needs of the college. Morale is generally high amongst most staff. Relationships amongst most members of the staff are satisfactory.	Leadership is reactive only. Morale is low amongst some staff. Relationships between staff are difficult.	Leadership is unaware of modern developments. Morale is low amongst most staff. Staff relationships are demoralised and ineffective.
Accountability is generally achieved at all levels.	Accountability is poorly administered at all levels.	Accountability is poor throughout the college.
There is a calendar of programme team meetings. Quality control is being achieved in many areas of activity. Performance data is used and recorded for major programme components.	Teams rarely meet to discuss the needs of study programmes. Quality control is poor in many areas of work. Performance indicators are collected but not used.	Teams see no need for meetings. Quality control is not effectively carried out. Performance indicators are not used.
Lines of communication throughout the college are generally good.	Lines of communication are inadequate	Lines of communication do not work in practice.

4. Unsatisfactory, i.e., showing some major shortcomings as listed in (5) below, in important areas.

5. Poor, i.e., showing many of the following shortcomings:

- no strategic plans
- no consideration of departmental plans
- short term planning only
- staff are not informed of future developments
- forecasts ignore data and trends
- college structure does not work effectively in practice
- senior management are not respected by the college staff
- staff are not properly deployed in their duties
- leadership is unaware of modern developments
- morale is low amongst most staff
- staff relationships are demoralised and ineffective
- accountability is poor throughout the college
- teams see no need for meetings
- quality control is not effectively carried out
- performance indicators are not used
- lines of communication do not work in practice.

An alternative approach for developing a grade descriptor can be made by reference to Table 2.1 in which a series of gradations facilitate the determination of the quality judgement.

Staffing

Characteristics

Teaching staff are a college's most valuable resource. They are also the most expensive and must therefore be carefully deployed. A programme of study needs a group of teachers with different experiences who adopt a variety of methods in teaching and directing students. They require the generalists who can teach many subjects up to a certain level, the specialists whose expertise has been developed through research and those who have an up-to-date knowledge as practitioners to support vocational programmes of study. It is also sensible to ensure that the teaching team has an appropriate age and gender profile. Departments need to maintain an up-to-date audit of their skills and competences as a basis for providing continuing education programmes, consultancy and research.

The numbers of teachers involved must be sufficient to meet the overall aims of the programme of study. These will include full-time, part-time and those on fractional appointments or at associate lecturer status in addition to service teachers from other academic subject areas in the college. The actual numbers of teachers involved will vary depending upon the programme of study and the central themes of the curriculum. They must be sufficient to meet the tutorial and assessment criteria laid down in the programme of study documents. Where there is an over reliance on part-time teachers, programme commitments are often over stretched. The teachers must be appropriately qualified in their respective subjects and should have spent some time developing teaching skills. Teachers on vocational programmes should also have relevant previous industrial or commercial experience, and have undertaken updating or secondments where this is necessary. On higher level programmes it is desirable that teachers have research and consultancy experience. In these cases their research students and assistants are able to contribute to tutorials, assignments, demonstrations and other classroom based activity.

Efficiency

There have been rapid changes in programme delivery during the late 1980s, and these will continue to meet to meet new demands of the 1990s. These include the increase in student numbers with funding at the margins in order to reduce unit costs. The simplest measure of efficiency is the students to staff ratio (SSR). This indicator has a long history and is widely applied internationally because it is fairly straightforward to calculate and because it measures indirectly the costs of a programme of study. However, there is no clear link between SSRs and quality. For purposes of comparison, SSRs are analysed by discipline groups that are broadly:

Group 1 Laboratory based programmes

Group 2 Classroom based programmes

In further education (FE) the SSR is, on average, 12.5:1 (1992) although due to student absenteeism and drop out rates the actual value is often much lower. For classroom based Programmes of Study the SSR may be as high as 18:1. In higher education (HE) the SSRs for classroom based programmes are not untypically 20:1, and it is not exceptional for these to be as high as 30:1. Laboratory based courses in HE have SSRs of approximately 12:1.

Care needs to be exercised when calculating the SSR, since different formulae are used to suit different circumstances. In the simplest examples the full-time student numbers are divided by the full-time teachers. However, colleges that have only these classifications are rare. With students attending programmes in different modes of study taught by teachers who are employed full-time and part-time, it is necessary to find the full-time equivalent (FTE) numbers. Ratios are used but are subject to change to meet new circumstances. Examples of these are shown in Table 2.2.

Table 2.2: Programme attendance ratios

Full-time students	= 1.00
HE sandwich students	= 0.90
FE sandwich students	= 0.75
Part-time students	= 0.40
Block release students	= 0.60
Evening only students	= 0.20
Short course students	= 1.10

Other measures also need to be considered in these calculations, such as the average student hours (ASH) attendance, the typical teacher's workload measured by the average lecturer hours (ALH) and the average class size (ACS). The Department For Education (DFE) monitors this data on an annual basis. Table 2.3 indicates the current trends:

Table 2.3: Measures of classroom efficiency (DFE 1993)

	1986/87	1987/88	1988/89	1989/90	1990/91
SSR					
HE	10.1	10.1	12.1	12.3	12.9
FE	10.6	10.8	11.3	11.8	12.4
ACS					
HE	15.1	15.3	14.2	14.3	14.8
FE	14.4	14.3	14.5	14.7	15.3
ALH					
HE	15.2	15.3	15.8	16.1	16.2
FE	18.1	18.1	18.1	18.4	18.5
ASH					
HE	23.1	23.5	18.7	18.7	18.6
FE	24.6	24.1	23.3	23.1	22.8

The following example shows typical calculations for SSR, ACS, ALH and ASH:

HE Department: 300 FT students (2x3 year courses, i.e., 50 students per year)

400 sandwich students (2x4 year courses, i.e., 50 students per year)

200 part-time students (2x5 year courses, i.e., 20 students per year)

The department employs 27 full-time teachers and the equivalent of 3 part-time teachers.

The SSR is then determined as follows:

$$\frac{300 + [400 \times 0.9] + [200 \times 0.4]}{27 + 3} = \frac{740}{30} = 24.66$$

Regardless of how these students are taught, the SSR will remain the same. In order to increase the efficiency, as measured by the SSR, either more students need to be recruited or fewer teachers employed. For example, assume that (i) each full-time student has a 'formal' attendance pattern of 15 hours each week (for 30 weeks), (ii) sandwich students attend for a similar period of time whilst in college and, (iii) part-time students attend for one day each week for 6 hours of tuition, then the total teaching hours, if each group is taught separately, are:

Full-time: 3 years x 2 groups   = 6 x 15 hours = 90 hours
Sandwich: 3 years x 2 groups   = 6 x 15 hours = 90 hours
    (Note one group is always in industry)
Part-time: 5 years x 2 groups   = 10 x 6 hours = 60 hours
                                    Total teaching = 240 hours per week

This provides an average lecturer hours (ALH) of 8 hours per week (240 hours/30 teachers). This excludes any allowance for supervision of the sandwich students who are working in industry. The average student hours (ASH) and average class size (ACS) can be calculated as respectively 12.56 and 33.63. This model can be adjusted and, in practice, the calculation will be more complex due to the use of seminars and tutorials.

However, using the simplified model, if it is desirable to reduce the duplication of teachers to different groups and to encourage more students to undertake self-study, the model can be adjusted. For example, if the first years were taught together then this would have the following effect: ACS 48.66, ALH 7.16, ASH 12.56 and SSR 24.66. The average student hours and the SSR remain unchanged. In practice, cancelled lectures and students' non-attendance has the effect of reducing the ASH and the SSR.

Support staff

Academic support staff include; administrators, secretaries and technicians. There is a trend to employ more staff in these categories and fewer teachers to provide cost savings and increases in efficiency. More expensive teachers are often employed on routine activities and duties that could be undertaken by less highly paid support staff. A trend is emerging to employ better qualified technicians to supervise students in workshops and laboratories, and administrators for the more routine management of academic programmes of study. This allows teachers more time to pursue scholarly activities and student instruction and tutoring.

Table 2.4: Support staff ratios

	FE Range	HE Range
Technician to FTE lecturer:		
Workshop based programme	1:2–1:4	1:3–1:6
Laboratory based programme	1:3–1:6	1:4–1:6
Classroom based programme	1:8–1:12	1:8–1:10
Administrator/secretary to FTE Lecturer	1:15–1:20	1:8–1:12

Using the quality grade descriptors given in Chapter 1, the following characteristics are used to judge the quality of the staffing in a college:

1. **Very good**, i.e., showing many of the following good characteristics:

- sufficient number of specialist staff
- good balance of different specialist disciplines
- use of external specialists
- well qualified academically
- policy and emphasis on the development of teaching skills
- all staff have chartered body status
- good and up to date industrial or commercial experience
- variety of teaching experience
- wide involvement with external examining and validating bodies
- all teachers are known specialists with up to date knowledge
- well graded age profiles
- appropriate ratio of males and females across most grades
- appropriate numbers of support staff
- well qualified and experienced technician staff
- good use of administrators

- sufficient secretarial support.

2. *Good,* i.e., showing some of the characteristics listed in (1) above, with no major shortcomings.

3. *Sound but undistinguished,* or good characteristics balanced by shortcomings:

- overall staff numbers are adequate
- minimum mix of different disciplines
- some use of part-time specialists
- appropriately qualified staff
- some development of teaching skills
- staff are professionally qualified
- industrial or commercial experience of staff is appropriate for range of programmes
- few staff have any experience of teaching elsewhere
- only a small percentage of staff have experience of moderating or examining other programmes
- staff have appropriate specialist expertise
- age profile standard and understood
- gender profile matches that of current students
- adequate number of support staff, appropriately experienced.

4. *Unsatisfactory,* i.e., showing some major shortcomings, as listed in (5) below, in important areas.

5. *Poor:* i.e., showing many of the following shortcomings:

- numbers of staff are insufficient
- types of subject disciplines are restrictive
- no part-time staff appointments
- academic qualifications are inadequate
- policy on teaching skills does not exist
- few staff are members of any professional body
- industrial or commercial experience of staff is negligible or not relevant
- teaching experience elsewhere is limited

- staff are either too inexperienced or have no interest in courses in other colleges
- staff have little expert knowledge of their subjects
- age profile is not recorded or known
- no policy on addressing any gender imbalances
- lack of adequate technician or support staff.

An alternative approach for developing a grade descriptor can be made by reference to Table 2.5 in which a series of gradations facilitate the determination of the quality judgement.

Staff Development

Staff development is about investing in people. It originates from a policy that reflects a college's aims and priorities. It is embraced in a plan that lists the detailed objectives whilst reflecting the needs and requirements of the college, department, programme of study and the members of staff. The plan includes the support staff as well as teachers. Staff development needs to be monitored by the central management in the college, but the responsibility for its implementation occurs at department level, although many colleges now use full-time staff development and training tutors. Some of the staff development initiatives will be identified by college managers or through national priorities, such as European awareness and information technology. The isolation, for example, of research activity from the programmes of study is generally unsatisfactory. Activities should be perceived as a continuum with linkages to project work, specialist modules, and so forth. Others will be derived from the programme of study teams and individual lecturers. In a proactive college or department, the needs will always outweigh the possibilities, due to both financial and time constraints. Some process and guidelines of prioritisation are therefore required to deal with these on a planned rather than ad-hoc basis. The analysis of requirements in the first instance may be derived from the staff appraisal system and programme of study teams. Thus the needs of individuals can be negotiated or balanced against the broader needs of the college, department and its programmes. The following are indicators of staff development activity:

Table 2.5: Staffing		
	Very Good:1	*Good: 2*
Sufficiency	Sufficient number of specialist staff. Good balance of different specialist disciplines. Use of external specialists.	Overall staff numbers are adequate. Adequate range of different disciplines. Good use of part-time teachers.
Qualifications	Well qualified academically. Policy and emphasis on the development of teaching skills. All staff have chartered body status.	Good academic qualifications. Some staff have teaching certificates. Most teachers are members of an appropriate chartered body.
Experience	Good and up to date industrial or commercial experience. Variety of teaching experience. Wide involvement with external examining and validating bodies. All staff are known specialists with up to date knowledge.	Relevant industrial or commercial experience. Some staff have teaching experience in other institutions. Some staff are involved as external examiners. Staff are seen as experts in their subjects.
Age & Gender	Well graded age profiles. An appropriate ratio of males and females across most grades.	Good distribution of ages. Policy of providing an appropriate gender profile.
Support Staff	Appropriate numbers of support staff. Well qualified and experienced technician staff. Good use of administrators. Sufficient secretarial support.	Adequate numbers of support staff. Qualified and experienced technicians. Sufficient administrators and secretarial support staff.

Table 2.5: Staffing		
Satisfactory: 3	*Unsatisfactory: 4*	*Poor: 5*
Overall staff numbers are adequate. Minimum mix of different disciplines.	Numbers of staff are inadequate. Inadequate range of specialist disciplines.	Numbers of staff are insufficient. Types of subject disciplines are restrictive.
Some use of part-time specialists.	Poor use of part-time staff.	No part-time staff appointments.
Appropriately qualified staff.	Academic qualifications do not match the courses.	Academic qualifications are inadequate.
Some development of teaching skills.	Teaching skills are not properly developed.	Policy on teaching skills does not exist.
Staff are professionally qualified.	Insufficient numbers of staff are members of professional bodies.	Few staff are members of any professional body.
Industrial or commercial experience of staff is appropriate for range of programmes.	Industrial or commercial experience of staff is limited or dated.	Industrial or commercial experience of staff is negligible or not relevant.
Few staff have any experience of teaching elsewhere.	Teaching experience is restricted.	Teaching experience elsewhere is limited.
Only a small percentage of staff have experience of moderating or examining other programmes.	No staff have external experience of other programmes.	Staff are either too inexperienced or have no interest in courses in other colleges.
Staff have appropriate specialist expertise.	Staff have limited expertise in their subjects.	Staff have little expert knowledge of their subjects.
Age profile is standard and understood. Gender profile matches that of current students.	Age profile is skewed. Gender is stereotyped to past expectations.	Age profile is not recorded or known. No policy on addressing any gender imbalances.
Adequate number of support staff; appropriately experienced.	Limited number of support staff. Few with appropriate expertise.	Lack of adequate technician or support staff.

- numbers of staff involved over three years: 80 per cent
- funding per FTE teacher: £250 per annum
- external funding as a percentage of SD activities: 15 per cent
- publications per FTE teacher: 2–3 per year
- attendance at courses and conferences: 80 per cent over three years
- secondments: Industry/Other education/College 30 per cent over three years
- capability with IT: proficient 20 per cent; competency 75 per cent.

The different activities will be:

- monitored for their effectiveness, e.g. through the services that the college provides and its implications for student learning
- evaluated for their specific contribution towards improving the overall performance of staff
- used for feedback to other staff
- used to make audit of qualifications, experience, skills, knowledge, etc. on an annual basis against the development plan and targets
- differentiated between the experienced, inexperienced and part-time staff. All new college staff are provided with an induction programme and mentor.

Staff appraisal

Staff appraisal must be considered as a prerequisite to the effective development of all staff. In some organisations it seeks to relate an individual's performance to pay (PRP) and is used to provide a better analysis for promotion. Most staff appraisal systems initially require the completion of a pro-forma that outlines individuals' achievements during the previous reporting period, their future needs, career developments, and immediate and long term objectives which relate to their job description. Most appraisal systems are programmed annually. The appraiser, who is often a head of department or senior member of staff, assesses an appraisee's performance against predetermined and agreed criteria. It will also include a course of action to be followed during the following year. In the case of teachers, the criteria will relate to:

- teaching performance
- programme administration
- programme development
- research and consultancy
- publications
- staff development activities.

A good staff appraisal system will:

- be brief in terms of the paperwork
- rely upon all relevant evidence
- be non-confrontational
- be based upon clear guidelines for procedures
- provide for a clear course of action
- be simple to administer
- include recommendations.

Using the quality grade descriptors given in Chapter 1, the following characteristics are used to judge the quality of the staff development of the college:

1. *Very good*, i.e., showing many of the following characteristics:
   - clear written policy at college and departmental levels; full implementation
   - appropriate funding to satisfy policy demands
   - use of external funding sources
   - annual staff appraisal and inputs from boards of study
   - use college, department and individual needs
   - wide range of activities
   - involvement by all staff
   - enhancement of the college reputation
   - good recording systems and evaluation of outcomes
   - effects upon programme delivery
   - evidence in programme monitoring

- innovation in the curriculum
- substantial income from grants, consultancy and intellectual property.

2. *Good,* i.e., showing some of the good characteristics listed in (1) above with no major shortcomings.

3. *Satisfactory:* i.e., sound but undistinguished, or good characteristics balanced by shortcomings:

- *ad-hoc* staff development plan within the constraints of future programme needs
- modest budget but able to support a few prioritised proposals
- informal discussions with staff to determine priorities which are largely restricted to the needs of programmes of study
- modest range of staff development
- insufficient recording, evaluation and dissemination
- sharing on an informal basis amongst close associates only
- effects of staff development can show improvement but not carefully monitored
- moderate income from these activities.

4. *Unsatisfactory,* i.e., showing some major shortcomings as listed in (5) below, in important areas.

5. *Poor,* i.e., showing many of the following shortcomings:

- no staff development plan records or achievements
- insufficient funding available to support even a meagre programme
- no recognition that staff interviews are relevant
- no staff development to evaluate or assess
- no impact upon either teaching or learning or curriculum developments.

An alternative approach for developing a grade descriptor can be made by reference to Table 2.6 in which a series of gradations facilitates the determination of the quality judgement.

Accommodation

The initial impression gained by any visitor to a college is created by the layout of the site and its buildings. However, it is necessary to distinguish carefully between the physical characteristics and the way that the premises are managed. The primary aspects of the former are:

- location
- type
- amount
- condition.

It is also necessary to determine whether the:

- size of rooms being used matches the student group size
- rooms being used are appropriate for the intended activity
- rooms are located adjacent to other related activities
- environmental controls are adequate
- overall condition of the decoration and displays are satisfactory
- accessibility for the disabled and sign posting is appropriate
- safety associated with certain types of activities is adequate
- premises are clean and tidy
- type, quality and suitability of the furniture is appropriate.

The management of the accommodation also needs to be appraised in respect of how well the space is used, for example:

- deployment through sensible timetabling
- furniture arrangement to suit the activity
- weekly room utilisation
- supportive and stimulating learning environment
- model of vocational practice.

Capacity

The DES (1984) has set down guidelines for the appropriate amount of space required. These recommend areas varying be-

Table 2.6: Staff development		
	Very Good: 1	*Good: 2*
Policy	Clear written policy at college and departmental levels; full implementation.	Policy available but not fully implemented in practice.
Funding	Appropriate level of funding to satisfy policy demands; use of external funding sources.	Funding is appropriate to general needs but with reliance upon internal funds only.
Management	Annual staff appraisal and inputs from boards of study use college, department and individual needs.	Annual staff development interviews with some inputs from boards of study.
Outcomes	Wide range of activities. Involvement by all staff. Enhancement of college reputation. Good recording systems and evaluation of outcomes.	Range of staff development activities. Most staff are involved. College reputation is enhanced. Good recording systems. Evaluation of outcomes.
Impact	Effects upon programme delivery. Evidence in programme monitoring. Innovation in the curriculum. Substantial income from grants, consultancy and intellectual property.	Some impact upon programme delivery. Evidence in programme monitoring. Income from research and consultancy.

tween approximately seven square metres and thirteen square metres per FTE student. The areas required are dependent upon the activities being undertaken and the type and level of programmes offered. However, the recommendations are apt to become outdated as new methods of study evolve. In most cases the overall spatial requirements are now less, as formal teaching hours have reduced to allow students take more responsibility for meeting the learning requirements of their programmes of study. The DES also sets out area standard guidelines for the amount of

Table 2.6: Staff development		
Satisfactory: 3	*Unsatisfactory: 4*	*Poor: 5*
Ad-hoc staff development plan within the constraints of future programme needs.	Reactive staff development but without any consideration of future needs.	No staff development plan records or achievements.
Modest budget but able to support only a few prioritised proposals.	Some funding available but not used, or targeted on unsuitable development.	Insufficient funding available to support even a meagre programme.
Informal discussions with staff on future priorities which are largely restricted to needs of programmes of study.	No formal structure used to prioritise staff development.	No recognition that staff interviews are relevant.
Modest range of staff development. Insufficient recording, evaluation and dissemination.	Too few staff undertake any identified forms of staff development. Activities not evaluated.	No staff development to evaluate or assess.
Sharing on an informal basis amongst close associates only. Effects of staff development can show improvement but not carefully monitored. Moderate income from these activities.	No sharing of staff development results. Little or no evidence of effects upon teaching and learning or programme developments.	No impact upon either teaching or learning or curriculum developments.

teaching space required by each student. For example, in a typical classroom, each student requires about two square metres. This compares with as little as one square metre in a purpose built lecture theatre and as much as five square metres in a laboratory. In heavy craft workshops, such as engineering or construction, the recommended area is approximately eight square metres per student.

Table 2.7: Typical room area ratios (DES 1984)

	Typical areas per student (square metres)
Lecture theatres	1.0
Classrooms	1.8–2.1
Laboratories	3.0–4.6
Art & design studios	3.2–5.6
Construction/engineering	7.5–8.4

After staff costs, premises-related expenditure is the next most significant item in a college's budget. These costs include rates, heating, lighting, cleaning and the general running costs associated with the maintenance of the buildings and site. Many of these elements are fixed costs bearing little relationship to their actual usage. Thus, if the volume of activity can be increased – in most colleges this is occurring – the unit cost or cost per FTE student reduces.

Utilisation

The utilisation of the accommodation can be monitored against national norms or the college's target figures. In order to compare this, it is first necessary to prepare an inventory of the available accommodation and then measure the actual usage.

- What room space is available *(seats)*
- When this space is available *(frequency)*
- How this space is used *(occupancy)*.

For example: a lecture theatre capable of seating 100 students is available for 40 hours each week. During a typical week it is in use for 30 of these hours and on average is occupied by 70 students. The utilisation factor is:

$$\frac{30 \times 70}{40 \times 100} = 0.525 \text{ i.e. } 52.5\%$$

College managers expect that space should be used for about 80 per cent of the time at 80 per cent capacity, i.e., 64 per cent utilisation. Accommodation plans are often based upon this indicator. Student drop-out rates, cancelled and rearranged lectures means that achieved utilisation is, in reality, closer to 49 per cent, i.e. usage factor 70% at a capacity of 70%.

Efficiency

The colleges that provide for a large proportion of part-time students, adult education or evening short courses operate their premises on a three session five days per week basis. Days are typically of twelve hours' duration. Some colleges open parts of their premises, such as libraries, at weekends, work to an extended college year and encourage summer schools to use their accommodation in order to achieve greater efficiency.

An examination of room utilisation data shows that there is a dramatic reduction in the need for teaching accommodation between 1200 and 1400 hours and that a significant decline in use occurs after 1500 hours, particularly later in the week. This trend is less pronounced in colleges where a significant amount of adult education occurs. Figure 2.2 represents a day's activity in a typical college showing the hourly needs for accommodation.

Condition

A large proportion of the accommodation used by colleges was built either at the turn of the twentieth century or during the large educational buildings programme of the 1960s. Only a limited amount of systematic maintenance has since been undertaken and consequently a good deal of building stock is in a poor condition. The 'Hunter and Partners' survey carried out for the former Polytechnics and Colleges Funding Council (PCFC) estimated that over £600m needed to be spent on the buildings in that sector. Additional sums of money are also required for the other further and higher education colleges. Condition monitoring is a concept which is concerned with comfort for those who use the premises and includes decorative order, heating and ventilation, lighting, sound and acoustics, type of furniture, cleanliness, ambience, ease of access and location, displays and artefacts to help create a stimulating learning environment.

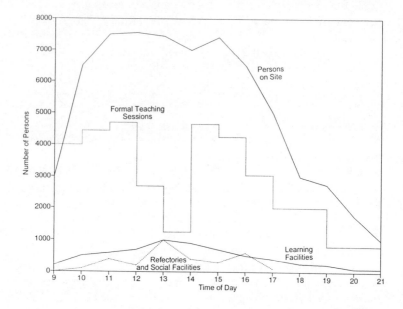

Figure 2.2: A day's activity in a typical college

Future developments

In assessing the suitability of the accommodation, it is necessary to take into account the probable and possible developments for its use. These may include:

- changes in teaching and learning styles
- movement towards large group teaching
- the 'reading' for a degree and the importance of self-supported study.
- the needs for study skills and open access workshops
- an extension of the opening times of the premises especially the library and other learning resources
- resource based learning developments.

Colleges have accommodation policies and systems that are used for reviewing and evaluating the accommodation. The policies include:

- information on changes in health and safety regulations
- maintenance programmes
- suitability for current use
- links with other accommodation for flexibility
- innovation
- cost
- overall effectiveness.

Using the quality grade descriptors given in Chapter 1, the following characteristics are used to judge the quality of the accommodation of the college:

1. *Very good*, i.e., showing many of the following characteristics:
- purpose design and use
- specialist accommodation
- specialist laboratories that fulfil health and safety requirements
- appropriate room shape
- ease of location
- good storage space, particularly for hazardous substances
- good state of repair
- recent decoration
- clean and tidy
- welcoming and stimulating
- good room layout
- carpeting
- good acoustics and sound controls
- good temperature and ventilation
- good levels of lighting
- comfortable seating

- modern and matching furniture
- equipped: overhead projector (OHP), audio-visual aids (AVA), chalkboards
- match to class sizes
- high utilisation and match to tasks being undertaken.

2. *Good*, i.e., showing some of the good characteristics listed in (1) above with no major shortcomings.

3. *Satisfactory*: i.e., sound but undistinguished, or good characteristics balanced by shortcomings:

- acceptable standard, general fitness for purpose
- some specialist laboratories that fulfil health and safety requirements
- shape and size of rooms are appropriate
- location is accessible
- adequacy of storage space with provision for hazardous materials
- state of repair is acceptable
- decoration has been carried out in the past seven years
- room is properly cleaned
- welcoming but lacking stimulation
- room layout is traditional
- utilitarian; floor tiling
- adequate sound and noise controls
- adequate temperature controls
- lighting is appropriate to the tasks being performed
- standard desks and chairs
- equipped OHP and chalkboards
- general match to class and room sizes
- utilisation at norm levels
- suitable for tasks being undertaken.

4. **Unsatisfactory**, i.e., showing some major shortcomings as listed in (5) below, in important areas.

5. **Poor**, i.e., showing many of the following shortcomings:
- overall standards are poor
- room is not suited to the tasks being undertaken
- no laboratories
- health and safety requirements are not met
- poor shape and size of rooms affect learning
- location results in wasted time for staff and students
- little storage space
- no provision for hazardous materials
- room has structural damage
- decoration over 15 years ago
- room is scruffy
- dispiriting and dismal
- room layout is discouraging to learning
- badly worn or bare floor
- external noise and poor acoustics
- room suffers from extremes of cold and heat
- poor lighting which could result in eye strain
- furniture is dilapidated and broken
- no equipment and poor quality and size of chalkboard
- mismatch between rooms and students
- room is used infrequently
- no planning of room allocation.

An alternative approach for developing a grade descriptor can be made by reference to Table 2.8 in which a series of gradations facilitate the determination of the quality judgement. Clearly care must be used in the application of Table 2.8. For example, a poor quality room which is used infrequently may not be a substantial handicap provided that other accommodation is readily available.

Table 2.8: Accommodation		
	Very Good: 1	*Good: 2*
Fitness & Purpose	Purpose design and use.	Standard accommodation.
	Specialist accommodation.	Fitness for purpose.
	Specialist laboratories that fulfil health and safety requirements.	Specialist laboratories that fulfil health and safety requirements.
	Appropriate room shape.	Appropriate room shape.
	Ease of location.	Ease of location.
	Good storage space particularly for hazardous substances.	Good storage space particularly for hazardous substances.
Maintenance	Good state of repair.	Good state of repair.
	Recent decoration. Clean and tidy.	Decoration is good. Clean and tidy.
Ambience	Welcoming. Stimulating. Good room layout.	Welcoming. Stimulating. Suitable room layout.
Comfort	Carpeting. Good acoustics and sound controls. Good temperature and ventilation.	Carpeting. Acoustics and sound controls. Acceptable temperature and ventilation.
	Good levels of lighting.	Appropriate lighting.
Furniture Equipment	Comfortable seating. Modern furniture. Matching furniture. Equipped: OHP, AVA. Chalkboards.	Comfortable seating. Modern furniture. Equipped: OHP, Chalkboards.
Management	Match to class sizes.	Match to class sizes.
	High utilisation.	Good utilisation.
	Match to tasks being undertaken.	Suitable for tasks being undertaken.

Table 2.8: Accommodation		
Satisfactory: 3	*Unsatisfactory: 4*	*Poor: 5*
Acceptable standard. General fitness for purpose. Some specialist laboratories that fulfil health and safety requirements. Shape and size of rooms are appropriate. Location is accessible. Adequacy of storage space with provision for hazardous materials.	Unsatisfactory standard. Not suited to the tasks being undertaken. No specialist laboratories that fulfil health and safety requirements. Shape and size of room are inappropriate. Location is difficult to access. Inadequate storage space.	Overall standards are poor. Room is not suited to the tasks being undertaken. No laboratories. Health and safety requirements are not met. Poor shape and size of rooms affects learning. Location results in wasted time for staff and students. Little storage space. No provision for hazardous materials.
State of repair is acceptable. Decoration has been carried out in the past 7 years. Room is properly cleaned.	Room has some surface damage. Decoration is grubby. Dirty and untidy.	Room has structural damage. Decoration over 15 years ago. Room is scruffy.
Welcoming but lacking in stimulation. Room layout is traditional	Uninviting and ageing. Layout of room is inappropriate to the tasks being undertaken.	Dispiriting and dismal. Room layout is discouraging to learning.
Floor tiling. Adequate sound and noise controls. Temperature controls are adequate. Lighting is appropriate to the tasks being performed.	Worn floor covering. External noise and poor internal acoustics. Controls are lacking in some features. Lighting is not satisfactory for the work being done.	Badly worn or bare floor. External noise and poor acoustics. Room suffers from extremes of cold and heat. Poor lighting which could result in eye strain.
Standard desks and chairs. Equipped: OHP. Chalkboards.	Variety of furniture, some of which is in poor condition. Lacking in any equipment. Unsatisfactory chalkboards.	Furniture is dilapidated and broken. No equipment and poor quality and size of chalkboard.
General match of class and room size. Utilisation at norm levels. Suitable for the tasks being undertaken.	Room and class sizes are poorly matched. Room utilisation is low. Inappropriate use of specialist rooms.	Mismatch between rooms and students. Room is used infrequently. No planning of room allocation.

Equipment

In assessing the quality of specialist equipment the overriding consideration is one of fitness for purpose. The equipment must be:

- adequate for the numbers of students using the equipment
- suitable for the range of activities being undertaken
- of a broad range in order to offer variety of learning.

Suitably located equipment facilitates maximum utilisation; this is helped when the equipment is appropriately managed and maintained by qualified technicians. The departmental ownership of equipment must not be permitted to impede its greater efficiency by refusing use to students from other departments who may be on different programmes of study. Open access arrangements offer students as wide an opportunity as possible for their own learning. The maintenance and replacement of equipment are interrelated and rolling programmes will be available by way of inventories showing purchase costs and dates, repairs and servicing and life expectancy. In respect of the latter, there is much equipment in colleges that has already exceeded these expectations. The high replacement costs of major items of equipment have become prohibitive and place a heavy burden on public funds. This is confirmed by the equipment model for the replacement of capital equipment in a construction department, shown in Appendix 4. Other sources of funding will need to be sought, or arrangements with nearby industry may be able to provide the appropriate demonstrations and experiments to allow students' access beyond normal working hours.

Workshops and laboratories

Workshop and laboratory accommodation are required in many different subject areas from science through to construction. They are used for designated purposes within programmes of study and are often unsuitable for activities other than those for their designed purpose. Workshops may be composed of large open spaces for practical tasks, such as those connected with the building industry. They may include high cost industrial standard machinery in the case of engineering or intricate laboratory equipment in physical science. Workshops and laboratories, as teaching areas, should be fit for the purpose, based on the characteristics specified for accommodation in Table 2.8.

Workshops and laboratories also incur expenditure for consumable materials and the replacement of small hand tools. This is typically about £150 per FTE student for engineering and construction crafts. Schemes of work designed to make the best possible use of materials through ingenuity in the design of projects and the recycling of the materials are essential. Space is also required adjacent to the workshops for the removal of rubbish and waste materials.

Using the quality grade descriptors given in Chapter 1, the following characteristics are used to judge the quality of equipment of the college:

1. *Very good*, i.e., showing many of the following characteristics:
   - written policy on present and future needs
   - inventory of equipment
   - rolling programme for replacement and enhancement
   - priority listing
   - model for future funding needs
   - funding allocation for maintenance and upgrading
   - external sources of funding
   - sufficient to match student group sizes
   - appropriate in range and type
   - ratio of students to equipment assists learning
   - equipment is modern and up-to-date; some represents state of the art; all conforms to industry standards
   - accommodation modern and spacious
   - space requirements for students and safety meets laid down criteria

- equipment has good utilisation factors
- technician support skilled
- equipment is routinely and well maintained
- students are allowed good and reasonable access
- facilities are well cared for.

2. *Good*, i.e., showing some of the good characteristics listed in (1) above with no major shortcomings.

3. *Satisfactory*: i.e., sound but undistinguished, or good characteristics balanced by shortcomings:

- rolling programme for the replacement of some equipment
- funding available on a repair and maintenance basis
- consumables only at an adequate level through careful planning
- adequate to meet student needs, but some over-sharing of equipment
- limited in range and type of equipment
- equipment conforms with dated industry standards
- space requirements comply with nationally agreed standards
- accommodation is adequate
- equipment is well utilised
- technician support is only adequate
- maintenance is adequate
- access is generally restricted to set times.

4. *Unsatisfactory*, i.e., showing some major shortcomings as listed in (5) below, in important areas.

5. *Poor*, i.e., showing many of the following shortcomings:

- no policy or rolling programme
- no funding is available for equipment
- some is out of commission due to lack of repair

- funding for consumables restricts experiments and projects
- curricula are restricted due to a lack of suitable working equipment
- equipment is approaching obsolescence, does not entirely meet current regulations for safety
- there is restricted access and movement
- environment is not conducive to good practice
- equipment use is not recorded
- technician support is not helpful to students
- management responsibilities are unclear.

An alternative approach for developing a grade descriptor can be made by reference to Table 2.9 in which a series of gradations facilitates the determination of the quality judgement. As with other judgements, care must be used. For example, first class equipment is of little advantage if students cannot gain access to it.

Computing

The key criteria for information technology facilities are that they are accessible and up-to-date. In addition to being used for timet-abled classes, the facilities should be available for individual stu-dent's use. The facilities need to be available throughout the day and evenings and weekend accessibility is also desirable. The ratio of students to computers varies depending upon the nature of the programmes of study and the modes of attendance. A ratio of 25:1 is now unlikely to offer the appropriate level of support for stu-dents. A ratio of about twelve FTE students to each computer is desirable at the present time, and ratios of 8:1 are becoming more common as independent learning requirements develop.

Most computing rooms offer pleasant working conditions with specially designed furniture and adjustable height chairs. Hard-ware equipment must be modern, noting the rapid changes and developments that have occurred in the past few years. Comput-ing equipment over five years old is usually obsolete. The hard-ware capability must offer students the availability of modern software, with general purpose software installed on the machine.

Table 2.9: Equipment and resources		
	Very Good: 1	*Good: 2*
Policy	Written policy on the present and future needs. Inventory of equipment. Rolling programme for replacement and enhancement. Priority listings.	Written policy. Inventory. Rolling programme for replacement only.
Funding	Model for future funding needs. Funding allocation for maintenance and upgrading. External sources of funding.	Some allocation of funding for replacement. Adequate funds for consumables.
Quantity	Sufficient to match student group sizes. Appropriate in range and type. Ratio of students to equipment assists learning.	Appropriate to meet students' needs but restricted in terms of variety.
Quality	Equipment is modern and up to date: some represents state of the art. All conforms to industry standards.	Majority of the equipment is modern. Industry standards are met.
Space	Accommodation is modern and spacious. Space requirements for students and safety meets laid down criteria.	Accommodation is up to date and space requirements meet all criteria.
Management	Equipment has good utilisation factors. Technician support is skilled. Equipment is routinely and well maintained. Students are allowed good and reasonable access. Facilities are well cared for.	Utilisation is high. Technician support is appropriate. Maintenance is adequate. Access is available to students at all reasonable times. Facilities are well cared for.

Table 2.9: Equipment and resources		
Satisfactory: 3	*Unsatisfactory: 4*	*Poor: 5*
Rolling programme for the replacement of some equipment.	Limited rolling programme or inventory. No priority listing.	No policy or rolling programme
Funding available on a repair and maintenance basis. Consumables only at an adequate level through careful planning.	Insufficient funds for either upgrading or replacement. Consumable materials are inadequate.	No funding is available for equipment. Some is out of commission due to a lack of repair. Funding for consumables restricts experiments and projects.
Adequate to meet current student needs, but some over-sharing of equipment. Limited in terms of range and type of equipment.	Extensive sharing of equipment by students. Some equipment is not available.	Curricula is restricted due to a lack of suitable and working equipment.
Equipment conforms with dated industry standards.	Much of the equipment is out-dated and does not meet industry standards.	Equipment is approaching obsolescence, does not entirely meet current regulations for safety.
Space requirements comply with nationally agreed standards. Accommodation is adequate.	Insufficient space is available to allow students adequate working space and ease of operation.	There is a restricted access and movement. The environment is not conducive to good practice.
Equipment is well utilised. Technician support is only adequate. Maintenance is adequate. Access is generally restricted to set times.	There is a poor utilisation of equipment. Access for students is restricted to class sessions. Technician support is inadequate and they are poorly trained. There is no co-ordination of resources.	The equipment use is not recorded. Technician support is not helpful to students. Management responsibilities are not clear.

A range of specialist software for particular subject disciplines is also essential. In addition to manufacturers' user guides and other documentation, support is required from technicians and teachers to advise on the use of the hardware and the software. 'Help' systems will have been installed onto the computer hardware.

The college will have an agreed, regularly updated policy and development plan for computing. This will address college-wide strategies, accommodation requirements, the replacement of equipment and its enhancement to meet the needs of particular programmes of study in a college. There will be a rolling programme for these developments. The computer facilities will be well co-ordinated centrally but also allow for specialist installations where these are necessary. The *ad-hoc* purchasing of information technology (IT) equipment within departments is discouraged, since this rarely fits within an overall college policy. Colleges' IT committees are composed of members from the different departments, to agree the long term policy, curriculum needs and funding requirements.

Library

A comparatively large amount of work has been done on the identification of performance indicators for library services. In addition to computerised catalogues, libraries have computer systems that are capable of producing data on stock usage, the proportion of stock on loan, loans per item of stock and the number of items per reader. In the larger libraries this information, together with the number and types of enquiries that are made, are used to inform on future decisions regarding the longer term directions of a library service. Information is also available on the way that the library service meets, or fails to meet, the needs of the users. Table 2.10 sets out the more useful indicators that are used for the evaluation of these learning resources.

Table 2.10: Library indicators
(Council of Librarians in Higher Education)

	per FTE students	
	FE	HE
Floor area (sq. m.)	0.1–0.3	0.5–1.0
Seating (No)	0.03–0.07	0.1–0.3
Area per seat (sq. m.)	4–8	5–10
Bookstock (No)	7–17	30–80
Bookstock expenditure (£ per annum)	5–20	15–80
Opening hours (weekly)	42–50	55–70
Library staff (No)	0.06–0.09	0.09–0.12

The quality of the library provision is assessed on:
- size and quality of accommodation
- seating/study capacity
- amount of current bookstock
- periodicals provision
- amounts spent on new bookstock
- staffing levels; grades, full-time and part-time
- opening hours
- user committees.

References

Council of Librarians in higher education *Annual statistics.*

Department of Education and Science (1984) *Assessing the capacity of further education buildings, Design note 37.* London: Department of Education and Science, Architect's and Building Branch.

Department of Education and Science (1990) *Higher education in the Polytechnics and Colleges: Construction.* London: HMSO

Department For Education (1993) *Student: staff ratios and unit costs at grant maintained Further Education establishments in England: 1990/91.* Statistical Bulletin 5/93. London: Department For Education.

Further Reading

Department For Education (1992) *Further education and sixth form colleges; Development strategies for accommodation.* London: Department For Education, Architect's and Building Branch.

Further Education Unit (1989) *Towards an educational audit.*

HMI Invitation Conference (1989) *In pursuit of quality: an HMI view. Quality in Higher Education.* Heythrop Park Proceedings, June.

Chapter 3

Students and Their Support

> Support services can always prove success by showing service to someone... not necessarily you.
>
> *Douglas Evelyn*

General Issues

The work of student support and associated services needs to be regularly monitored and evaluated in order to improve what is often already good practice. The evaluation of the processes involved will lead to an enhancement in practice through:

- college management and organisation
- needs relating to staff development in these areas
- development of performance indicators
- demands of students.

The student support services must be professionally organised and easily accessible, informative and capable of meeting the individual needs of students. Students should feel that the support provided by the college staff will be available at all reasonable times and be provided with sympathy and guidance.

Students' Response to Quality

Students are the main clients of further and higher education colleges. Their views are valuable and can contribute to improved satisfaction levels for programmes of study and other activities which enhance the overall college reputation. The views of employers, the government, parents and the academic community will bring different priorities to bear upon services and expertise that are provided. The students' response to quality is reflected in the:

- quality of their experiences
- quality of services and functions which are provided
- level and currency of their achievements.

The level of satisfaction of students on programmes of study in further or higher education will vary depending on the individual student him or herself: their personalities, motivation, friends and ambitions. Satisfaction also depends upon the appropriateness of the learning programme for which they have applied and been selected, how well they are coping with the programme and their place within it. The location of the college and the comfort criteria factors associated with their study and domiciles are also important ingredients. The arrangements made by the college and the programme of study team for managing their experiences will represent major contributions to their satisfaction. Students' experiences can be broadly summarised as follows:

Personal factors:

- relationships between a student and other students and the influence of these relationships on self-image and self-esteem
- relationships with tutors
- domestic arrangements
- financial aspects
- desire to study
- short and long term benefits and opportunities.

Programme of study factors:

- first choice programme
- type of programme
- timetabling
- work content and arrangements
- ease, challenge and success
- arrangement of assignments
- completion and level of award
- relationships with tutors and other staff.

College factors:
- type of college
- location; geographical, city centre
- condition of buildings and equipment
- access to facilities
- recreation and similar.

The following are issues which need to be addressed by a college:
- improvement of the students' lifestyle
- motivation of students for study
- creation of student contentment
- assisting students in their quest for knowledge and learning
- achieving successful outcomes for students.

Careers Guidance

It is desirable, but insufficient for the output or achieved qualifications and other aspects of a programme of study to be generally worthwhile, for the teaching to be of a high standard. It is also important that the programme of study and the individual students enrolled on it are well matched. The students need the necessary aptitude and motivation to complete the programme of study successfully. Successful completion rates across a wide range of courses from Advanced (A) level, Business and Technology Education Council (BTEC) and first degree are typically only about 70 per cent. Completion rates are much less than 70 per cent on some programmes. When students select a programme of study instead of, for example, the preferred possibility of employment, the successful completion rate can fall to as low as 40 per cent. Guidance in secondary schools after taking the General Certificate of Secondary Education (GCSE) examinations is sometimes inadequate for students, other than those choosing the traditional route of A-levels. Poor practice includes failure to identify clearly and honestly the various options that are available to students, other than staying on at school. The correct emphasis of linking funding with student enrolments may result in more students being incorrectly advised when leaving school. Whilst most schools and colleges have a named individual responsible for careers, surveys (Ofsted 1993) have shown that:

- their work is often poorly co-ordinated
- their training varies widely
- their contact with other staff is sometimes little more than routine
- good guidance is based upon firm data relating entry and output qualifications
- the options to formal schooling are not clear.

Recruitment and Enrolment

Links

The links between schools, colleges and employers are often not sufficiently well developed. These links also need to be extended and strengthened with overseas colleges. In assessing the quality of the links the following aspects are considered:

- length of time the specified links have been in place
- importance of links with other colleges or schools
- development of these links
- benefit the students gain from such links
- involvement of the programme team
- frequency of visits to the feeder schools or colleges
- benefits to feeder colleges and schools
- efforts expended.

Marketing and publicity

Colleges' publicity includes a main prospectus, individual programmes of studies brochures, advertising in the national and local newspapers, as well as in specialist periodicals and journals. Factors that are considered are:

- effectiveness of the different kinds of publicity
- information and presentation of the publicity
- areas that are targeted and their limits
- cost-benefits of the publicity

- feedback from students on programme
- way in which most students find out about college programmes
- use of open days as a means of marketing.

Using the quality grade descriptors given in Chapter 1 the following characteristics are used to judge the quality of the marketing and liaison in the college:

1. Very good, i.e., showing many of the following characteristics:
   - effective marketing of services
   - well targeted information
   - detailed knowledge of client groups
   - informative and attractive publicity
   - involvement with local and national media
   - proactive in new ventures and developments
   - clear evaluation of strategies
   - schools' links programmes or activities for all abilities
   - established network between FE and HE colleges
   - franchised programmes
   - programmes of exchanges with overseas institutions through funding agencies
   - involvement with trade or professional bodies at local and national levels
   - established long term links with local and national industry and commerce
   - joint venture schemes and sponsorships with commerce and industry
   - balanced and active advisory services
   - recognised reputation for excellence
   - high levels of external funding
   - well supported continuing education programme
   - many staff involved with validating and examining bodies.

2. Good, i.e., showing some of the good characteristics listed in (1) above with no major shortcomings.

3. Satisfactory: i.e., sound but undistinguished, or good characteristics balanced by shortcomings:

- marketing of all services are appropriate
- information reaches client groups
- good knowledge of most client groups
- acceptable level of publicity and information
- some involvement with the media
- basic level of response to new initiatives
- minimum evaluation of strategies
- some schools' links programmes
- links between FE and HE are broadly in line with national initiatives
- franchised programmes restricted to major subject areas
- links with institutions abroad are on a personal basis only
- a few staff are involved with trade or professional bodies
- links with commerce and industry related to student employment
- some *ad-hoc* consultancy
- advisory service meets several times each year
- programme provision is generally satisfactory
- limited financial support from external sources
- good but limited continuing education programme
- a few staff are involved with external bodies.

4. Unsatisfactory, i.e., showing some major shortcomings as listed in (5) below, in important areas.

5. Poor, i.e., showing many of the following shortcomings:

- little attempt is made to market the college or its programmes
- college relies upon clients' enquires only
- no information is maintained
- publicity information is inadequate

- no media involvement
- little in the way of reactive or proactive responses
- strategies are not evaluated
- no schools' links programmes
- no links between FE and HE
- no plans for any form of franchising
- no plans for any links with overseas colleges
- staff have no interest in being involved with outside bodies
- links with industry and commerce are poor
- consultancy has not been envisaged
- advisory committees are not thought necessary
- programmes have a poor reputation
- external funding has not been considered
- no plans for continuing education
- staff have not considered external body membership.

An alternative approach for developing a grade descriptor can be made by reference to Table 3.1 in which a series of gradations facilitate the determination of the quality judgement.

Applications

Applications received by colleges are analysed: by total number, trends, types, non-standard entry, widening access, and so forth. For a particular programme of study or group of programmes of study the following performance indicators are important:

- the number of applicants per place
- whether this is increasing or decreasing
- the evolving pattern between full-time and part-time enrolments
- the types of students, grades and subjects
- the type of student who performs better; this is sometimes not understood by programme of study managers
- the acceptance of students from a wide range of social, economic and academic backgrounds.

Table 3.1: Liaison and marketing		
	Very Good: 1	*Good: 2*
Marketing	Effective marketing of services. Well targeted information.	Effective marketing of services. Carefully targeted information.
	Detailed knowledge of client groups. Informative and attractive publicity and information.	Global knowledge of client groups. Informative and attractive publicity.
	Involvement with local and national media. Proactive in new ventures and developments. Clear evaluation of strategies.	Involvement with local media. Proactive response to new initiatives. Good evaluation of strategies.
Links	Schools' links programmes or activities for all abilities. Established network between FE and HE colleges. Franchised arrangements.	Schools' links programmes. Developing links between FE and HE colleges. Some franchised programmes.
	Programmes of exchanges with overseas institutions through funding agencies. Involvement with trade or professional bodies at local and national levels.	Formation of links with institutions abroad. Several staff involved with trade or professional bodies at local and national levels.
Industry & Commerce	Established long term links with local and national industry and commerce. Joint venture schemes and sponsorships with commerce and industry. Balanced and active advisory services.	Good links with local and national industry and commerce. Consultancy links with commerce and industry. Active advisory services.
Other	Recognised reputation for excellence. High levels of external funding.	Wide reputation of quality provision. Some levels of external funding.
	Well supported continuing education programme.	Good continuing education programme.
	Many staff involved with validating and examining bodies.	Some staff involved with validating and external bodies.

Table 3.1: Liaison and marketing

Satisfactory: 3	*Unsatisfactory: 4*	*Poor: 5*
Marketing of all services are appropriate. Information reaches client group.	Marketing is not co-ordinated Information fails to reach wide client groups.	Little attempt to market college or programmes. College relies upon clients' enquiries only.
Good knowledge of most client groups. Acceptable level of publicity information and presentation. Some involvement with the media. Basic level of response to new initiatives. Minimum evaluation of strategies.	Basic knowledge of only the main client groups. Poor quality information in content and presentation. Little involvement with the media. Generally reactive to new situations. Strategies are inadequately evaluated.	No information is maintained. Publicity information is inadequate. No media involvement. Little reactive or proactive responses. Strategies are not evaluated.
Some schools' links programmes. Links between FE and HE are broadly in line with national initiatives. Franchised programmes restricted to major subject areas. Links with institutions abroad are on a personal basis only. A few staff are involved with trade or professional bodies.	Schools' links provision is restricted. Links between FE and HE are only in a limited number of subject areas. Plans for franchising at an early stage of development. Links with any institution abroad under consideration. Staff are not involved with their trade or professional bodies.	There are no schools' links provision. There are no links between FE and HE. No plans for any form of franchising. No plans for any links with overseas colleges. Staff have no interest in being involved with outside bodies.
Links with industry and commerce are related to student employment. Some *ad-hoc* consultancy. Advisory service meets several times each year.	Few members of staff are involved with industry and commerce. Consultancy has not been considered. There are no advisory committees.	Links with industry and commerce are poor. Consultancy has not been envisaged. The need for advisory committees is not thought to be necessary.
Programme provision is generally satisfactory. Limited financial support from external sources. Good but limited continuing education programme. A few staff are involved with external bodies.	Programmes are not well thought of. No external funding. No continuing education programme. Staff are not involved with external agencies.	The programmes have a poor reputation. External funding has not been considered. No plans for continuing education. Staff have not considered external body membership.

Selection

The selection process examines how quickly applications are dealt with and the criteria that are used to accept or reject students. There is still discrimination towards students, more prevalent in higher education, who do not fit easily into the prescribed entry pattern of programmes of study. The selection process is based on a model of previous students' success patterns and considers the following:

- college's analyses of previous students' completions and successes

- identification of student satisfaction indicators against applicants

- use of systems such as ALIS (A-level Information Service), to correlate students' performance

- factors used to reduce student drop out and non-completion rates

- models tested and developed to ensure improved performance, success and satisfaction.

Students' non-completion rates are too high, even in the United Kingdom, where the academic criteria for selection are rigorous and more specific than in many other European countries. However, funding patterns must not expect non-completion rates to be zero, otherwise colleges will restrict entry only to those who are sure of success. Such a model would then reduce students' opportunities. Improved methods of student profiling, at all levels, through a records of achievement system, provides a better match between potential students and future outcomes. Where students are not recruited to a chosen programme due to non-selection, perhaps on academic grounds, then colleges should offer alternative study programmes based upon the student's potential. Foundation courses or a series of modules to bring students up to the required level for enrolment to their chosen programme of study should be available.

Accreditation of Prior Experience and Learning (APEL)

Historically and traditionally, in order to progress to the next level in the education system, a student needed to have the prescribed entry requirements. In higher education this often meant A-level qualifications, although vocational qualifications have become more recognised as a means of entry as students opt for this route. There are many examples of students who, without the formal entry qualifications, have been able to succeed on programmes which were, in the past, supposedly beyond their reach. The introduction of General National Vocational Qualifications (GNVQ) should result in a parity with traditional academic qualifications. In an attempt to increase the numbers of those who might benefit from higher education the widening of access has also been introduced. Students can be credited with prior learning or knowledge that has not been acquired in the traditional manner. Students' records of achievements (ROA) or profiles are able to indicate a breadth of experience and life skills which can be used as an alternative means of entry to programmes of study other than by the academic or named routes. The following should be considered:

- the ability and motivation that are necessary to complete a programme successfully
- the flexibility of a programme of study's entry requirements
- the redesign of programmes to allow for widening access
- the credits given to students who have already achieved an appropriate level of proficiency in specified subjects.

Student Contracts

Student contracts assure those entering courses that, if they fulfil their part of the agreement, the college will endeavour to complete its part by improving their chances of success. The college's part of the contract includes:

- a summary of the equal opportunities policy
- an expectation that students will make the best use of the available facilities
- a commitment by the students to a responsible attitude towards learning and personal development
- providing individual action plans
- assigning each student to a personal tutor

- records of achievement on completing the programme of study
- an outline of the year's work at the beginning of the programme
- using a variety of teaching and learning methods
- assessing and returning coursework within a specified time
- informing students on their progress at least once per term
- providing workshop support for literacy, numeracy and information technology
- writing references
- making provision for a European language where this is not a part of the programme
- providing access to computing facilities with learner support.

Students must undertake their own part of the contract by committing themselves to:

- taking responsibility for their learning
- giving proper consideration to others in the college
- respecting the college and its facilities
- adopting responsible behaviour
- accepting a personal programme of study
- attending and taking part in all teaching sessions
- meeting deadlines for coursework submissions.

The following considerations are evaluated in respect of student contracts:

- the fairness to both parties
- its possibility of achievement by all students
- that it is progressive
- that the college facilities keep pace with the increases in student enrolments and needs.

Induction

The transition to a new programme of study in a new environment is not easy for many students. It must therefore be made as smooth as possible. The students' link with their personal tutors should take place as soon as possible after accepting a place on the programme. This tutor will be the student's main point of contact throughout the student's period of study. During the induction process students will need to gain information about the college, its services and further details appertaining to the programme of study. The induction process will:

- introduce the students to the programme team
- provide students with a programme of study handbook
- outline the weekly timetable, the importance of attendance at all formal class meetings and the need to keep up-to-date with assignments
- include aspects of students' safety, health and welfare
- state where help can be obtained in case of difficulties
- provide the relevant details of the skills workshops
- include supervised visits to the various learning resource centres
- introduce aspects of study skills
- arrange for meetings with the student union representatives.

The induction process may require a full week to allow students to familiarise themselves with the layout of the college and its environs and gather the necessary information that will help them throughout their studies. The colleges which provide for a good induction process will provide clear indications of requirements and expectations and this will help to settle the students into college life. The following are considered:

- that the induction process is well managed to meet the needs of the students
- that it provides students with the appropriate information
- that it offers support to students who may require other study skills

- that in addition to the giving of information it includes some diagnostic work.

Programme of Study Handbooks

Programme of study handbooks identify:
- college; facilities; organisations, leisure, recreational
- staffing; qualifications, main teaching subjects, research interests, room and telephone number, times of availability
- useful contacts; library, counsellor, health centre, accommodation officer
- description and aims of the programme of study; structure and content
- curriculum; formal contact with staff, lectures, seminars, tutorials, projects
- attendance requirements; monitoring
- supporting or optional study subjects; guidelines
- timetable; available before the start of term or semester
- assignments; number per subject, dates for submission and return to students; written criteria; worked solutions
- examination timetable with dates
- assessment criteria; simplicity, regulations
- career opportunities and guidance
- programme of study committees and advisory boards
- examination boards; external examiners, results, progression, referral, failure, appeals procedures
- reading lists; sent with the offer of a place on the programme of study.

Annual supplements to the handbook are provided for students in the subsequent years of the programme, identifying changes that have occurred since they enrolled. The better handbooks offer a comprehensive set of information, including the students' contract and, where appropriate, photographs of the staff. Programme of study handbooks are evaluated on their:

- presentation
- content
- relevance
- usefulness
- ease of use
- general readability.

The Tutorial System

Programmes of study have developed tutorial systems for administrative, personal development and regulatory purposes. The programme tutors or directors are responsible for the overall management. They are assisted in their roles by the year tutors who are responsible for a single year of the programme and personal tutors who are responsible for individual students. The actual role of these different tutors varies, but the following functions or tasks must be undertaken. In some colleges, departmental managers have been appointed to deal with the routine administrative matters, thereby allowing teachers more time for carrying out academic work. The personal tutors are responsible for offering guidance and help to students and in resolving problems and difficulties. The following tutorial tasks are performed:

Administrative:
- registration and progression
- student attendance control (use of smartcards)
- monitoring and feedback of performance
- preparation and updating of action plans
- student references
- changes of address or programme.

Personal development:
- development of student's study skills
- promotion of self-awareness and self-image
- encouragement of personal development
- consolidation of basic skills

- promotion of critical intelligence
- social skills.

Regulatory (disciplinary):
- creation of sense of order
- acceptance of responsibility
- minimise anti-social behaviour.

Staff development and tutor training help to make the tutorial systems more effective and enable individual teachers to have a greater awareness of their roles and responsibilities. It has somewhat surprisingly been observed that teachers and students sometimes do not know their personal tutees and tutors, respectively. It is now common to find as many as twenty tutees to a single tutor and, with increases in student enrolments, this ratio is expected to become higher. Where part-time students are involved, due to the full-time equivalent ratios that are used, the tutor/tutee ratios are even higher, although the responsibility for the student's welfare is shared with the employer's representative. Many personal tutors have only a passive tutor role which is activated when difficulties arise. In some colleges where the SSR has been observed to be as high as 30:1, the personal tutors have a difficult task in carrying out their duties and responsibilities properly and effectively. In colleges that have chosen to employ a smaller proportion of full-time teachers the situation is exacerbated. In some colleges second year students are paid to run weekly sessions for first year students. Their main task is to encourage them to organise their work effectively and to discuss approaches to problem solving. The better personal tutors have an interest in their tutees' well-being, have a good knowledge of them from the student records system and through personal contact and expect to meet them formally at least once per academic term. Evidence indicates that if students sought advice on their problems earlier, or these were more easily identified, then fewer students would become demotivated and leave their programmes of study prematurely. The student's attendance on programmes can be maintained with an improvement in their performance. The good personal tutor is always likely to be the first point of reference for the student in case of difficulties arising. Where more expert advice is required, colleges have experienced counsellors available or are able to call upon outside agencies, such as:

- the chaplaincy
- health services
- financial advisors
- legal assistance
- welfare service.

A good tutorial system will be able to identify the different needs and pressures which are experienced by students. It will be

- easily understood by teachers and students
- accessible
- helpful
- informative
- responsible
- reliable.

The quality of these roles and relationships include:

- knowledge of tutor roles
- knowledge of tutors/tutees
- frequency of meetings
- (simple) recording of meetings
- student action plans
- reduced withdrawal or non-completion rates.

It is also important to be aware of the following:

- a sufficiency of teachers to cope with anticipated problems
- that teachers have acquired the appropriate expertise
- their friendliness and helpfulness
- that problems get solved and eliminated
- that the same problems do not reoccur each year
- that the tutors are sympathetic to students' needs.

Personal Student Action Plans

The personal action plans prepared in co-operation with each student highlight the student's level of achievements and deficiencies, based upon their entry requirements and progression on the programme of study. It sets out a plan for the time that the student is on a college programme, and is revised at least once per academic year or semester. These plans can be conveniently divided into three parts:

Part A describes the student's acquired skills, abilities and achievements and provides a current picture that can be represented by a curriculum vitae:

- academic achievements
- any work experience
- hobbies and interests
- statement of health
- personal qualities.

Part B states the student's aims in educational and career terms, and the role of the college in helping to achieve them. The aims includes occupational and personal goals, the reasons for selecting the programme and their short and long term objectives. Any factors that might influence these outcomes would be listed. A skills level analysis would be provided for the main core areas.

Part C describes personal targets and the means of achieving them. The personal tutor is responsible for agreeing personal targets with the student and for their review and updating. Any items of concern such as late or outstanding coursework or poor attendance is recorded. This process helps to reduce the amount of discussion and time spent at the end of the academic year. The evaluation of action plans includes:

- their comprehensiveness
- their agreement with the student
- the frequency of updating
- individual preparation with the co-operation of each student
- provision of a good vehicle for objective progressing.

Credit Accumulation and Transfer Schemes (CATS)

Traditionally, further and higher education have operated closed systems of education. These have included: designated achievements at entry, prescribed periods of time, single modes of attendance, limited subject areas, specified subjects of study, based in a single college location and on a defined programme of study. Credit transfer systems were introduced in the 1970s to offer students different routes through their educational programmes, to allow for changes in their aspirations or changes in their careers. Credit transfer systems allow students the opportunity to transfer between different education and training routes. They also allow units to be combined in such a way as to provide general, specialist, academic and vocational programmes and allow a variety of approaches to learning. The schemes are aimed at broadening access in an attempt to offer wider educational opportunities to students without the formal entry qualifications, and to provide a means of entry to higher education for returning adults. The CATS were developed, in part, in response to the demographic decline, to increase students' participation rates and to offer some continuity where a student's education had been disrupted. Most schemes are based upon a points accumulation system of 120 points for a first year programme and 360 points for an honours degree. Some schemes also seek to recognise the completion of different stages of a programme of study by awarding a certificate or diploma to students, who may choose not to complete the whole programme. Issues relating to CATS include:

- whether another college will recognise the student's achievements
- the extent to which validating or professional bodies will offer recognition
- the quality control procedures employed
- the achievement of the appropriate range of units for further progression
- the achievement of units at the appropriate levels.

Equal Opportunities

The statutory framework defining discriminatory behaviour is provided by The Sex Discrimination Act 1975 (amended) and The Race Relations Act 1976. These acts define as unlawful both direct and indirect discrimination, and place a duty to promote equality of opportunity. The successful implementation of a policy will lie in:

- a commitment by the senior management of the college to a value system which sees human resource development as vital to the continuation of the organisation
- clear leadership in the implementation of this system within the value system
- firm and public support for the agreed policy within the value system
- real and adequate resources for the implementation of equal opportunities.

The following are the components of a good practice in equal opportunities:

- clear policy
- effective monitoring
- college marketing and selection which reflects policy
- strategies to recruit across traditional boundaries
- appropriate distribution of males, females and ethnic minorities
- the curriculum takes into account changing attitudes
- teaching modes and styles which are appropriate
- code which deals with sexual and racial harassment
- attitudes in the college reflect respect
- work experience employers observe the code
- access to facilities for students with disabilities.

Careers' Services

Careers services envisage that the acquisition of qualifications will be used to obtain employment or to continue on a further programme of education or training. The careers and counselling services guide students in personal, educational and vocational areas of activity. The major aim is to help the students to develop skills and abilities to become more effective in their adult life and career. Most colleges make use of outside agencies, such as the local careers' service, employers or other colleges in giving their advice to students. The activities for students include:

- understanding themselves
- development of knowledge and street credibility
- learning how to make positive choices in life
- being aware of education, training and career opportunities
- choosing a career, rewards, personal success and enjoyment
- managing the transition into adult life more effectively
- application to the work environment and voluntary service.

The better systems are proactive, recognising and responding to different student needs. This implies a series of learning experiences that offer progression, continuity and coherence and which form an integral part of the process of education and training. The service liaises with the different tutors by offering them the necessary support. The components of a good careers system include:

- careers' education including liaison with the national careers' service
- access to information about the world of work including publications and computer access such as The Educational Counselling and Credit Transfer Information System (ECCTIS)
- work experience which could include visits to commerce and industry, work shadowing, industrial simulation and placements
- recording of achievements in the development of personal action plans
- use of performance indicators such as:
  - ○ student destination data, analysed to provide indications of what students do

- the employment rate in the case of vocational programmes
- non-completion statistics showing ways that this is being remedied.

Student Welfare

In addition to the support services listed above, colleges provide a range of welfare services to enable the students to gain the maximum benefits from their programmes. These include:

Medical services

Health and nursing services are provided to offer a range of support from basic first aid facilities through to health education. Some of the latter exist as a result of student demand or due to the concern of medical staff about certain issues. The extent of the services varies from a reliance upon the services of a local medical general practitioner in the smaller colleges, to the full-time employment of nurses and doctors in the larger colleges. Surgeries are provided to suit the convenience of students and other valuable advice is provided on diet and general health matters.

Crèche facilities

These are required to provide suitable child minding services that are local and economical. Crèches are managed by nursery nurses in a ratio of about eight children per nurse. There is still a general under-provision of these facilities and this prohibits some individuals from study.

Chaplaincy

The chaplains in the larger colleges are normally full-time appointments. In the smaller colleges, local ministers of religion are employed on a part-time basis. It is usual to have an Anglican, Roman Catholic and free church minister. Other faiths will be involved to suit local circumstances. The advantage of the part-time appointments is that they are already employed in the local community.

Housing and other accommodation

Colleges offering full-time programmes in higher education provide halls of residence for students, although these cannot meet
the increased numbers of student enrolments. In addition, the
colleges' accommodation officers manage flats and houses for
private landlords and have recommended addresses in the private
rented sector and details of rooms in family homes. The costs of
accommodation prohibits some students from undertaking further study and unsuitable living environments cause some students to terminate their programmes of study. Colleges need to
provide clear guidance to students, from the outset, on the accommodation that is available, its quality and costs, together with an
idea of running costs and other living expenses. These represent
major items of expenditure to students. The accommodation officers are responsible for the availability of appropriate residences
and coping with students' housing problems throughout their
study programmes.

Health and safety

A college is responsible for ensuring, as far as possible, the health,
safety and welfare of its employees, students and members of the
public who may be affected by any of its activities. It must comply
with the Health and Safety at Work Act. In order to comply with
regulations and codes of practice, the provision and maintenance
of the following aspects are considered:

- plant, equipment and safe systems of work
- arrangements for the safe use of substances
- adequate instruction, training and supervision
- information on safety policies
- inspection and testing procedures.

All colleges have a safety committee through which policy is
formulated and improvements to current procedures can be implemented. Students must also take reasonable care for the health
and safety of themselves and for other persons who may be
affected by their acts or omissions. Students are required to wear
the protective clothing provided and access to laboratories and
workshops must only take place under adequate supervision.
Some members of staff will have been trained in rudimentary first

aid procedures, and notices around the college will state what needs to done in an emergency. The following are considered:

- the role of the college safety officer
- the number of incidents over the past five years
- magnitude of these incidents
- improvements in policy and practice
- general condition of facilities.

Finance and legal advice

Financial problems are a major burden for many students in further and higher education. It is recognised that the present personal funding arrangements for students' grants are barely adequate. In some cases this causes full-time students to obtain part-time work in the evenings and at weekends, diverting them away from their studies. For some students this affects their overall academic performance. Colleges have several provisions for dealing with student financial hardship and for providing financial advice and assistance when necessary. However, the possibility of receiving help in this way is small due the heavy demands placed upon the resources. The college is able to advise students on travelling expenses, student loans, tax relief for vocational qualifications, social security benefits, unemployment benefits, income support, child benefit and housing benefit. All colleges have a student access fund but, although funded by central government, it is insufficient to meet the needs of all students. The college staff are also able to advise on budgeting and debt and how and where to seek legal advice. The following are considered:

- the staff who are involved
- the training they receive
- the extent of the service that is provided
- whether programme and personal tutors are informed of their work
- the ease with which students receive help
- the way that the college monitors and evaluates these services.

Counselling services

Specialist counselling is provided by designated student counsellors. The ratio of counsellor to students varies but a recommended ratio is approximately 1:2000. Over 50 per cent of students referring themselves to the counselling service do so for issues related to their programme of study, such as choice of programme, study patterns and examinations. Personal issues such as adjusting to student life, separation from family, divorce and bereavement and sexual identity are other common reasons for referral (DFE 1993). Counselling services also make a significant contribution towards the needs of overseas students, ethnic minorities, students with disabilities and adult returners. Good characteristics include:

- setting clearly established goals for students and counsellors
- clear and shared understanding for any referrals
- maintenance of appropriate records
- preparation of an annual report which addresses the objectives and issues.

Student Unions

Student unions are able to play an active part in the provision of a range of student services, such as sporting and leisure activities and welfare services. Where good relationships exist between the union and the senior managers in a college, students benefit from improved services. Issues include:

- funding and accountability
- nature of activities undertaken
- services provided
- representation for all students, including those on part-time programmes
- relationship with institution managers.

Student Complaints and Grievance Procedures

The following are some of the major causes of dissatisfaction by students:

- poor quality of programme delivery
- poor timetabling arrangements
- lack of assignment schedules and the delay in the return of assignments
- lack of information on student performance
- limited access to learning facilities
- personal confrontation
- poor provision of college resources.

Some of these problems arise because of poor management, lack of experience, uncommitted programme team, clash of personalities or students' financial problems. All colleges have a grievance procedure under which students can raise complaints. The college objectives aim to:

- foster good relationships between the students and the college
- ensure that grievances are solved as quickly and fairly as possible
- provide access to the Principal or Vice Chancellor where, in the student's opinion, difficulties have not been dealt with adequately.

Questionnaires

Questionnaires are an effective way of eliciting feedback from students and employers on the quality of a programme. The questionnaires must be designed to ensure that responses from students identify the main issues that are involved. The questionnaires need to be completed by students at different stages during the programme, preferably biannually. The forms are sometimes referred to as students' perception of course (SPOC) forms. The first questionnaire and analysis is done after the first six weeks into the programme to gain the students' initial reactions and response to the programme. A second questionnaire is requested after the completion of the year's or semester's study. Further questionnaires are required at similar stages throughout the remainder of the programme. The employer's perception of the course (EPOC) also needs to be completed annually. The employers, who regularly employ students from a programme, will also be invited to complete questionnaires at major programme reviews in order to see how well the programme is suited to the needs of practice. The analysis of these forms provides the programme and college managers with a summary of students' and employers' perceptions; what is good, what is unsatisfactory, and what needs to be changed. The students must feel that the information that they provide in this way is carefully considered and notice is taken of their responses. The questionnaire should address the following:

- the content of the programme of study
- the effectiveness of the timetabling
- how well the programme is delivered
- the spacing of assignments, criteria referencing and their return to students within a reasonable time
- access to college resources
  - availability
  - quantity
  - suitability
- the general management of the whole process.

An example of questions that may be referred usefully to the students is given in Appendix 5. Students may also be required to complete questionnaires on teaching performance, which can be used in conjunction with the staff appraisal system in respect of individual teachers. These include the teacher's:

- general organisation
- approachability and helpfulness
- ability to lecture and organise tutorials and seminars
- their return of assignments and the helpfulness of their comments.

The answers to these questions will provide information on whether the facilities and systems which are provided by the college are adequate and available, how well the systems for ensuring the best delivery of the programme work out in practice and to what extent these meet the needs and aspirations of the students.

- improvement in student performance at GCSE and A-levels
- increase in the number of students with vocational qualifications
- increase in student age cohort participation rates
- reduction in the numbers of applicants to places on programmes of study, due to a wide expansion of the latter
- whilst student expectations and achievements will continue to increase, employment opportunities are unlikely to match these requirements.

Using the quality grade descriptors given in Chapter 1 the following characteristics are used to judge the quality of the students and services in the college:

1. *Very good*, i.e., showing many of the following characteristics:
   - well documented admissions policy
   - high demand for places on the programme
   - very high standard of entry qualifications
   - flexible entry for non-standard students
   - students with non-standard entry qualifications are encouraged to apply
   - programme is first choice for majority of applicants
   - attempts are made to redress any gender or ethnic imbalance
   - few student withdrawals and completion rates are high
   - effective guidance and counselling systems
   - proactive policies effected through personal tutor system
   - high quality induction process which covers all college and academic issues
   - comprehensive handbook which covers academic and college matters
   - routine monitoring of student feedback
   - students are given clear information on their performance

- students are involved in boards of study and other committees
- students enjoy the programme
- students are highly motivated
- records of attendance are kept and attendances are high
- students benefit from the skills obtained from their programmes
- students easily gain employment
- employers approach the college for their future employees.

2. *Good*, i.e., showing some of the good characteristics listed in (1) above with no major shortcomings.

3. *Satisfactory*: i.e., sound but undistinguished, or good characteristics balanced by shortcomings:

- well documented admissions policy
- adequate level of applications
- suitably entry qualifications to meet the demands of the programme
- often includes non-standard entry students
- few students choose the programme as a priority
- programme includes an appropriate mix of students
- average student withdrawal and non-completion rates
- guidance is appropriate to meet students' needs
- induction process which deals with the major issues
- handbook of essential information
- students receive feedback at regular but infrequent times
- students have few complaints
- most students enjoy the programme
- motivation of students is only average
- attendance of students is generally good
- employment prospects are generally good
- employers hold students from the programme in high regard.

Table 3.2: Students		
	Very Good: 1	*Good: 2*
Entry	Well documented admissions policy. High demand by students for places on the programme.	Well documented admissions policy. Demand for places on the programme is above average.
Qualifications	Very high standard of entry qualifications. Flexible entry for non-standard entrants. Students with non-standard entry qualifications are encouraged to apply. Programme is first choice for the majority of applicants. Attempts are made to redress any gender or ethnic imbalance.	High standards of entry qualifications. Recruitment includes students with non-standard entry qualifications demonstrating that the policy on access is effective. Many students choose the programme as a first option. An appropriate mix of students are encouraged to apply.
Retention	Few students withdraw from the programme of study and completion rates are high.	Low student withdrawal and non-completion rates.
Guidance	Effective guidance and counselling systems. Proactive policies effected through personal tutor system. High quality induction process which covers all college and academic issues. Comprehensive handbook which covers academic and college matters. Routine monitoring of student feedback. Students are given clear information on their performance. Students are involved in boards of study and other committees.	Students receive careful guidance through a good personal tutor system. Good induction process dealing with most aspects of the college and programmes of study. Good handbook covering all essential matters. Students receive feedback on their performance several times each term. Students have an input to the relevant committees.

Table 3.2: Students		
Satisfactory: 3	*Unsatisfactory: 4*	*Poor: 5*
Well documented admissions policy. Adequate level of applications.	The admissions policy is unclear. The level of applications fail to meet minimum targets.	There is no admissions policy. The programme often fails to recruit to target numbers and is run with low numbers or withdrawn.
Suitable entry qualifications to meet the demands of the programme. Often includes non-standard entry students. Few students choose the Programme as a first priority. The programme includes an appropriate mix of students.	Entry qualifications are either narrow or allow entry to students who are unlikely to stay on the programme or complete it successfully. Students select the programme as a fall back situation. Little attempt is made to recruit from an appropriate pool of students.	Entry qualifications are not clear allowing unrestricted entry, or entry from one source of supply. In general students are not matched to the course. Most students select the programme as a last resort. There is felt to be no need to address equal opportunities issues.
Average student withdrawal and non-completion rates.	High student withdrawal and non-completion rates and poor monitoring.	Student withdrawal rates either unknown or hidden. The non-completion rates are not monitored.
Guidance is appropriate to meet students' needs. Induction process which deals with the major issues. The handbook contains essential information only. Students receive feedback at regular but infrequent times.	Guidance is poor and misleading. Induction process is poor offering students little information on their programme. There is no handbook. Feedback to students is infrequent and not recorded.	Student guidance is either ineffective or non-existent. Students do not have an induction process. A handbook is believed to be unnecessary. Feedback is not provided until the end of the year.

Table 3.2: Students (continued)		
	Very Good: 1	*Good:2*
Motivation	Students enjoy the programme.	Students enjoy the programme.
	Students are highly motivated.	Students are well motivated.
	Records of attendance are kept and attendances are high.	Attendances at teaching sessions are good.
Employment	Students benefit from the skills obtained from their programmes and readily gain employment. Employers approach the college for their future employees.	Employment prospects for students are high. Employers are keen to interview students.

4. **Unsatisfactory**, i.e., showing some major shortcomings as listed in (5) below, in important areas.

5. **Poor**, i.e., showing many of the following shortcomings:
- no admissions policy
- programme fails to recruit to target numbers
- entry qualifications are not clear, allowing unrestricted entry or entry from one source of supply
- students are not matched to the course
- most students select the programme as a last resort
- equal opportunities are not addressed
- student withdrawal rates are either unknown or hidden
- non-completion rates are not monitored
- student guidance is either ineffective or non-existent
- students do not have an induction process
- handbook is believed to be unnecessary

Table 3.2: Students (continued)		
Satisfactory:3	*Unsatisfactory:4*	*Poor:5*
Students have few complaints.	Students complaints are not properly rectified.	Students make many complaints which are repeated from year to year.
Most students enjoy the programme.	Some students are unhappy with the programme.	Many students dislike the programme.
The motivation of students is only average.	Student motivation is poor.	Students have little or no motivation.
The attendance of students is generally good.	Student attendance is low.	Student attendance is poor and not properly monitored.
Employment prospects are generally good.	Employment prospects are traditionally low.	Few students are able to secure appropriate employment.
Employers hold students from the programme in high regard.	Employers do not prefer students from the programme.	Employers will not employ students from the programme.

- feedback is not provided until the end of the year
- students make many complaints which are repeated from year to year
- many students dislike the programme
- students have little or no motivation
- students' attendance is poor and not properly monitored
- few students are able to secure appropriate employment
- employers will not employ students from the programme.

An alternative approach for developing a grade descriptor can be made by reference to Table 3.2 in which a series of gradations facilitate the determination of the quality judgement.

References

Audit Commission and Ofsted (1993) *Unfinished Business: Full-time Educational Courses for 16–19 year olds.* London: HMSO.

Department For Education (1993) *Student Support Services in Higher Education*. London: HMSO.

Department For Education (Periodically) *Statistical Bulletins*. Department For Education

Further Reading

Further Education Unit (1991) *Developing Tutoring Skills*. FEU

Further Education Unit (1992) *Assessment of Prior Learning and Learner Services*. FEU

Chapter 4

Teaching and Learning

... they know enough who know how to learn.

Henry Brooks Adams

Lectures, Tutorials and Seminars

One of the biggest barriers to quality in further and higher education is poor teaching. Too often, teachers merely copy the techniques previously used by their own teachers. This practice tends to retard the progressive development of teaching techniques. The maintenance of a high standard of teaching can be helped by ensuring that teachers are appropriately trained, developed and appraised.

An extended study undertaken in further education shows the comparison (Table 4.1) between teachers who are teacher trained and those who are not.

Table 4.1: Grading of teaching sessions

	Very good	Good	Satis-factory	Unsatis-factory	Poor
Teacher trained	12%	47%	38%	3%	0%
Not teacher trained	8%	53%	28%	9%	2%

Although not statistically significant, Table 4.1 does indicate that a trained teacher gives a better overall performance than an untrained teacher; significantly, fewer classes are unsatisfactory or poor. The performance of part-time teachers tends to be more variable than full-time teachers and this often relates to the vetting and management of part-time staff.

The most commonly used teaching session is the lecture, which may be given to groups of between 15 and 250 students. It is one of the most economic methods of teaching, particularly for the larger numbers. With fewer students, a good deal of debate and verbal interchange can take place between teacher and students, if required, in which case the teaching sessions may cease to be a lecture and become a lecture-discussion. With large numbers, the transmission of information is almost entirely in one direction unless the teacher chooses to reinforce points in his or her presentation by sampling student opinion on a group basis by means of a co-ordinated response; in general, teaching sessions to large numbers are keynote lectures. There is no opportunity to test the students' understanding. To cope with decline of students' attention, it is important that the teacher, who may usefully exhibit the attributes of an actor, uses a variety of activity, for example the use of:

- audio/visual aids, demonstrations by means of artefacts and computer
- handouts, often incomplete, for completion by the students during the lecture
- individual problem solving techniques.

During the course of the presentation, it is expected that students are actively involved by means of supplementary note-taking and other relevant activities. In this way, students take responsibility for meeting the learning requirements of the teaching session (provided that the teacher does not undertake his or her presentation too quickly; this is a barrier to learning). Recording the material strengthens its recall and the record can be used to promote private study.

Other means of strengthening the students' understanding and recall can be made by:

- restating the learning materials in different ways
- providing references for the students to consult follow up material
- promoting student consultation, i.e., group dynamics.

Lectures are not as effective as other teaching sessions in promoting thought about a subject or developing attitudes. This is more easily undertaken by tutorial and seminar work.

Tutorials may be given by an individual teacher to numbers from one, that is, individual tutorial, to 15 students, that is, group tutorial. With smaller numbers of students, the tutorial is an expensive method of teaching. The tutorial can be designed to promote free group discussion or focus on problem solving. Too often tutorials are too large to achieve these objectives; with 20 or 30 students in attendance they are sometimes transformed into lectures. Many students are unable to benefit from the overcrowded session. Discussion is helped by an informal arrangement of the seating with the teacher not seen in an authoritarian role, apart from problem solving sessions in which the teacher helps an individual student or groups of students.

Seminars have characteristics similar to tutorials except that there is an initial presentation which is designed to focus the proceeding group discussion. It may be used at postgraduate or undergraduate level to promote an exchange of ideas and is usually more successful in the former unless the teacher exhibits considerable skill in handling the session. This may comprise:

- support and encouragement to persuade the students to contribute, particularly if it involves criticism of each other
- ensuring that the debate is relevant
- sensitivity when clarifying, elaborating and focusing on a seminal point
- listening and observing
- sharing leadership of the group with the student making the initial presentation
- acting a role depending on the needs of the seminar.

The role of tutorials and seminars should not be underestimated. The development of ideas and concepts is often through debate and the exchange of ideas. During the exploration of new ideas, students need to take risks with their learning. It is through debate that the process of critical and creative thinking is gradually developed. This development owes much to the skill of the teacher in managing small group work.

Practical Work

The facilities that should be available for students to undertake practical work are usually expensive in terms of equipment, accommodation, consumable resources and support staff. For example, undertaking engineering degree courses normally requires approximately £1000 per FTE student per year of subject specialist equipment. The better sessions are usually conducted with sufficiently small groups of students using pieces of equipment to enable all students to obtain hands-on experience. In this way, competence in the handling and use of equipment is obtained in addition to the interpretation of data, the relation of theory to practice, and the development of observation and group skills. Full scale work often simulates industrial practice and minimises inaccuracies. An increased use of information technology in laboratory activities reduces the need to carry out repetitive, time-consuming procedures thus enabling tasks to be carried out more quickly. Fieldwork is also in this category. Important features of practical work are:

- carefully planned sessions in which the practical session is preceded by the theoretical session
- clear instructions be made available at the start of the session.

More recently, there has been an increase in the use of demonstrations to larger groups of students. This is not as useful as hands-on experience but is helpful in some aspects – for understanding, for example, verification of basic assumptions used in analysis. Properly handled it can promote a measure of understanding, although only a few students may get an opportunity to undertake practical work. Limitations in the availability of facilities for practical work can result in the following shortcomings:

- students are unable to participate fully in learning activities through too many students having to use the same apparatus
- unavailability of equipment means that experience is not hands-on but acquired through demonstrations, videos or pre-printed notes
- insufficient equipment produces timetabling difficulties, resulting in theory and practice out of sequence – with practicals sometimes preceding theory

- students fail to achieve a closer, or deeper, knowledge of the subject due to lack of appropriate equipment to demonstrate theory and principles
- repetitive teaching has to be undertaken by the teachers because year group sizes are too large for the level of available equipment.

Overall, inadequate investment in equipment can lead to the delivery of some areas of the curriculum being unsatisfactory and this has limited the students' experience. However, the converse does not necessarily apply. Qualitative methods based on the standards of equipment alone are invalid. The equipment, however good, must be used correctly and outcomes must be appropriate. This depends on good teaching.

The use of project work is valuable in that the student is responsible for planning and conducting a piece of work from its inception to the written report. Students look deeply into the subject and integrate a number of different skills and disciplines to bring the project to fruition. These include:

- conducting a literature search
- designing the experiment
- interpretation of data
- organisation and presentation of work.

It is an example of student self-study activity par excellence. Team projects have a further advantage in that they develop group skills and give students an opportunity to gain insight into and understanding of the difficulties and complexities of a large project. In particular they impart an understanding of work undertaken by other members of the team, which gives a better value judgement of collaborative activities.

Independent Learning

From 50 per cent to 75 per cent of students' time which is allocated to the promotion of learning is spent working independently of the teacher. To maximise the benefits from the use of this time, the following characteristics and facilities must be present:

- the effective employment of self-study skills by the student

- open access study areas and learning resources; for example resources rooms, libraries, computer suites, language laboratories.

To promote learning, when a student and in later life, training and guidance in self-study skills is essential, most particularly for lower achievers who may not have discovered the techniques by which they learn efficiently. Emphasis should be placed on:

- study methods, for example SQ3R
- organising study time and working to schedules
- using the available learning resources effectively
- self-monitoring of study behaviour.

A key factor affecting learning is how a student perceives him or herself; in short, the self-esteem of the individual. The role of the tutor may be an important influence.

As students learn in different ways, a one-off session on self-study techniques for a large number of students as a preparation for a protracted programme of study is inadequate and may be of benefit only to a small number of those students. Counselling and reinforcement during the academic year is needed to integrate the effective development of self-study skills into the curriculum and the assurance that the student is employing those study skills. Some colleges have negotiated learning contracts with their students to emphasise the learning behaviour required by the student and learning support available from the teacher.

Important characteristics of a student centred study culture include:

- studio, tutorial and seminar work designed to encourage students to exercise a measure of self-sufficiency in undertaking their studies
- computer aided learning, computer simulation and open/distance learning arrangements
- students supplied with workbooks, video materials, etc., with inter-institutional co-operation undertaken to prepare subject learning materials on a co-operative basis
- emphasis placed on motivating students so that they develop an enthusiasm for learning which will continue through life.

The facilities required for independent learning may be comprised of a wide range of open access active and passive learning resources. For example: specialist book stocks; videos; tapes; tape/slides; computer suites; language laboratories. The design and availability of these facilities must be appropriate to cater for the demands of the students or some of their study time is ineffective. These design aspects are dealt with in detail in Chapter 2.

Attendance at Teaching Sessions

Students tend to use strategies that maximise their opportunities for success. Hence, teaching sessions that are beneficial in terms of learning or credit generation, for example laboratory sessions, are better attended than sessions in which the students judge that an appropriate level of learning fails to take place. Clearly, the mode of study can influence the overall attendance with part-time courses often less well attended than full-time courses due to the pressures of the work place on the part-time students. Nonetheless, in relative terms, the level of student attendance can often be an indicator of teaching quality. This trend is particularly noticeable at the less popular times during the day where the better teaching sessions still attract a good attendance.

Typical data from samples taken in further and higher education, Table 4.2, yield the following average percentages for attendance:

Table 4.2: Attendance at teaching sessions

Number of teaching sessions	Very good	Good	Satis-factory	Unsatisfactory factory	Poor
152	89%	80%	76%	70%	65%
113	70%	75%	63%	62%	-
18	93%	87%	80%	76%	80%

In sessions that are poorly attended, students who have failed to attend are often found engaged in other learning activities, for example assignment work, on a self-study or peer group learning basis, which they have judged to be more beneficial to progressing their studies.

Evaluation of Teaching Performance

Teachers are often sensitive to assessment of their work. Yet, many academic staff believe that good teaching is an important criterion in personal advancement in a career in academe. Teachers may be evaluated, directly or indirectly, by any or all of the following:

- heads of department
- students
- colleagues
- research output
- success rates of students
- students' coursework
- teachers' teaching materials.

Using the quality grade descriptors given in Chapter 1, the following characteristics are used to judge the quality of the teaching and learning in the college:

1. *Very good*, i.e., showing many of the following characteristics:
   - detailed scheme of work
   - expert knowledge of subject
   - reference to further reading and current publications
   - factually accurate and relevant and up-to-date information
   - appropriate pace, variety and enthusiasm
   - well presented demonstrations and explanations
   - stimulates thought and challenge
   - relates easily to students
   - monitors students' comprehension
   - good and wide use of visual aids and artefacts
   - well prepared and wide range of student handouts

- encourages a high level of student involvement
- students are engrossed in the activity
- students display a good level of understanding.

2. *Good,* i.e., showing some of the good characteristics listed in (1) above with no major shortcomings.

3. *Satisfactory:* i.e., sound but undistinguished, or good characteristics balanced by shortcomings:

- lesson plan
- essential level of subject knowledge
- little reference to further reading
- factually accurate but little reference to current practice
- lacking in a variety of activity
- demonstrations are adequately performed
- generally sound but lacking enthusiasm
- generally relates to students
- attempts to ensure students' understanding
- visual aids are used appropriately
- student handouts are clear in presentation and content
- limited discussion and student participation
- students are generally attentive
- most students cope adequately.

4. *Unsatisfactory,* i.e., showing some major shortcomings as listed in (5) below, in important areas.

5. *Poor,* i.e., showing many of the following shortcomings:

- no planning or scheme of work
- lacks appropriate knowledge
- incorrect references to further reading
- frequently factually incorrect
- no knowledge of current practice
- lacks enthusiasm, boring, inappropriate pace in delivery
- extensive use is made of dictation
- little demonstration or explanation where required

Table 4.3: Teaching and learning		
	Very Good: 1	*Good:2*
Preparation	Detailed scheme of work.	Scheme of work.
Knowledge	Expert knowledge of subject. Reference to further reading and current publications.	Thorough knowledge of subject. Reference to further reading and some further publications.
Presentation	Factually accurate, relevant and up to date information. Appropriate pace, variety and enthusiasm. Well presented demonstrations and explanations. Stimulates thought and challenge in students. Relates easily to students. Monitors students' comprehension.	Factually accurate and relevant and includes reference to current practice. Appropriate pace and some variety in presentation. Demonstrations are clear with good explanations. Stimulating and motivating to students. Relates to most students. Makes some checks on the students' understanding.
Teaching Aids	Good and wide use of visual aids and artefacts. Well prepared and wide range of student handouts.	Good use of visual aids. Good presentation of student handouts.
Response	Encourages a high level of student involvement. Students are engrossed in the activity. Students display a good level of understanding.	Many students are encouraged to be involved. Students cope well in discussions. Students show a sound understanding.

Table 4.3: Teaching and learning

Satisfactory: 3	Unsatisfactory: 4	Poor: 5
Lesson plan.	Poorly planned.	No planning or scheme of work.
Essential level of subject knowledge. Little reference to further reading.	Superficial level of knowledge only. No references to further reading	Lacks appropriate knowledge. Incorrect references to further reading.
Factually accurate but little reference to current practice. Lacking in variety of activity.	Sometimes factually incorrect, no reference to current practice, out of date. Disjointed delivery, dull.	Frequently factually incorrect. No knowledge of current practice. Lacks enthusiasm for the subject. Boring. Inappropriate pace in delivery. Extensive use is made of dictation.
Demonstrations are adequately performed. Generally a sound delivery but lacking enthusiasm. Generally relates to students. Attempts to ensure students' understanding.	Demonstrations are poorly organised and explained. Rudimentary delivery lacking in challenge. Is unaware of lack of rapport. No attempt is made to assess students' understanding.	Little demonstration or explanation where required. Lacking in stimulation and fails to motivate students. Relates poorly to students. Failure to ensure that students are comprehending.
Visual aids are used appropriately. Student handouts are clear in presentation and content.	No use made of visual aids. Handouts include errors and are poorly presented.	No visual aids available. No use is made of handouts.
Limited in discussion and student participation. Students are generally attentive. Most students cope adequately.	Some students are inattentive. Student activity is restricted to copying notes. Students have difficulties which are not met by the lecturer.	Students are disruptive and restless. High level of boredom with no response expected. Students display little or no understanding.

- lacking in stimulation and fails to motivate students
- relates poorly to students
- fails to ensure that students are comprehending
- no visual aids available
- no use is made of handouts
- students are disruptive and restless
- high level of boredom and no response expected
- students display little or no understanding.

The influence of accommodation, equipment and standards of work can be included by means of the integration process, as described in Chapter 1, using the relevant characteristics for these additional factors from Chapters 2 and 6.

An alternative approach for developing a grade descriptor for teaching and learning can be made by reference to Table 4.3 in which a series of gradations facilitate the determination of the quality judgement. Where appropriate, Tables 2.8, 2.9 and 6.4 can be used to include other relevant factors. An overall quality grade descriptor for a number of teaching and learning sessions can be determined by integration.

Table 4.3 shows the main characteristics that may be taken into consideration when judging the quality of teaching sessions, for example during teacher appraisal. Teachers who have the expertise to be able to generate the high levels of students' responses as shown in the bottom left hand portion of Table 4.3 are relatively few.

Yet another approach which has been used by the authors is that of an intelligent knowledge based, or expert, system to evaluate a quality grade descriptor. Appendix 6 shows the basic approach to setting up the system for teaching and learning using a LEONARDO shell. Similar techniques are used for the other activities and facilities.

Reference to Appendix 3 indicates that teaching staff, accommodation and equipment all correlate well with teaching and learning, i.e., 0.68, 0.87 and 0.80, respectively. The overall grading for an academic area correlates best with staff, i.e., 0.93. It is not unexpected that a good quality staff team is the key to overall quality. This is the basic assumption used by many visiting validation/accreditation teams.

Management of Coursework

The programme team is responsible for the organisation and management of the programme of study; this includes the design, as well as scheduling, and marking the coursework. There is a tendency for programme teams to set rather more coursework than they are able to handle effectively; consequently, even though the work may be well scheduled, which is not always the case, there is insufficient time for the marking and feedback to the students to be carried out effectively.

A prime motivator of students is the requirement for them to undertake work which is formally assessed and which counts towards their final assessments. Coursework has the added benefit of informing students of their progress on the programme of study, possible shortcomings and areas of work which need to be more thoroughly researched and understood.

The most important requirements may be summarised as follows:

- coursework designed to enable students to achieve the learning requirements of the programme
- encouragement for students to develop and use a variety of skills whilst undertaking the coursework
- well scheduled coursework programme in which bunching of assignments does not occur
- procedures which ensure that the coursework is quickly marked with a comprehensive feedback to the students on their individual and team performances.

Research

In many institutions research is believed to be 'a good thing', yet often there is no firm appreciation of its costs and benefits to an academic community either at departmental or institutional level. The taught programmes of study in a college are designed to transmit, to the students, knowledge that is already established and is believed to be conventional, i.e., orthodoxy. In contrast, research is an original investigation which is undertaken in order to gain knowledge and understanding. It does not include routine work which is designed to establish conventional conclusions, yet does include innovative consultancy work. Research investigations may lead to new techniques or artefacts; they may lead, through scholarship, to new or substantially improved insights. In some cases, the research can call into question the established orthodoxy. In extreme cases, few may be converted to the newly established orthodoxy and it will wait for a new generation to accept fully its value and adopt it.

Under these circumstances it is not surprising that the establishment of performance indicators to evaluate the research performance of an educational institution is controversial. Besides the use of professional knowledge and judgement by advisory panels to obtain an informed peer review, the following criteria are valid:

- publications and other identifiable outputs in the public domain
- citations
- success in obtaining research grants and scholarships
- success in obtaining research contracts
- number of research students
- completion rates of research students
- esteem indicators (Collins 1991).

(These criteria are set out in more detail in Appendix 7 in which a first stage performance indicator strategy for the quantification of research activity is suggested.)

Publications, which are clear evidence of research activity, are usually taken to include, in order of importance, publications in academic journals, professional journals, popular journals, books, reports, edited works and proceedings. Also relevant, particularly in departments in which a significant portion of the work is practical and applied, are patents and licences. Indeed, it is likely that groups of staff that are involved in this form of innovative activity are disadvantaged if publications in journals are used as the main criterion in judging research performance. It is wise to work secretly and patent sensibly when undertaking work capable of generating intellectual property; using the currency of journal publications places work in the public domain and hinders or prevents patenting.

The contribution of each of the publications to the overall research effort is weighted in accordance with its perceived level of importance. Comparisons within an institution are less of a problem than comparisons between institutions where rankings can be sensitive to the weightings; the movement of staff and multi-authored publications also cause difficulties. Much work has been done to measure the quality of work based on the frequency of citations (de Solla Price 1986); however, care has to be taken when considering examples of self-citation, uncomplimentary citations and staff mobility.

Research income is often considered to be an important indicator of research performance; which organisation is likely to fund research work which has no perceived market value, or potential market value? Although this method of measurement counts against researchers undertaking work in fields of activity in which funds are in short supply or where research does not require expensive equipment it is, nonetheless, difficult to play down the importance of substantial levels of research income. As research income often generates additional research workers, it is important to relate the income to the core of staff that produce the income. Indeed, as larger departments are likely to be more productive in terms of publications and income, these must be related to the number of research staff undertaking the work.

An important dimension of institutional quality is the successful completion of individual research programmes by postgraduate students. In some areas, completion rates are as low as 50 per cent even when taking into account significant extensions to the duration of the research programme. This is wasteful in resources and reflects poorly on the work of the supervisory teams and institutional management.

Finally, there is a number of factors that seem, at this stage, not to have a significant effect on research performance; for example, the SSR, average age of staff, investment in the library.

Influence of research work on the quality of teaching and learning

It is commonly believed that good researchers are also good teachers; yet there is little or no evidence that this is the case. Teaching and research are apparently independent abilities; just as it would not be usual that attaining the status of a professional researcher can be achieved without training, so it is with teaching. A good research department is considered to be a good teaching department, yet examination of the analysis in Appendix 3 shows that the correlation of research work with the quality of teaching and learning is not good, i.e., 0.08. At first sight this is surprising as it may be thought that teaching staff who are the most enthusiastic about gaining a greater insight into their subject areas would be the most enthusiastic teaching staff. However, unless a piece of research work is designed primarily to improve the quality of teaching and learning, and teaching staff fully understand strategies designed to promote good teaching and learning, it would be fortuitous if it did so.

In recent years, there has been a greater emphasis on improving the quality of teaching and there is an increasing opportunity to undertake scholarship designed to have an impact on teaching and learning, particularly the improvement of productivity through the more efficient delivery of teaching and more effective learning. Investigations (Teaching More Students Project 1992) have already been carried out in the following areas: problems and course design strategies; lecturing to more students; discussion with more students; assessing more students; independent learning with more students. In many cases there has been a concentration on enhanced courseware and the general use of new technology to improve the students' independent learning capabilities.

Just as there has been benefit in identifying staff who are responsible for undertaking subject specialist research, there is advantage in identifying staff whose prime responsibility is to undertake educational scholarship designed to improve teaching and learning strategies. This includes: improving student learning; development of mutual support within student groups; assessment techniques.

Management of research: research student and supervisor

Within the past decade or so it became clear that the completion record of research degree candidates left something to be desired. Most students failed to complete in an appropriate time period. Many did not actually write up their theses which meant that they failed to benefit from one of the more important aspects of research degree training despite the fact that they may have completed most other tasks satisfactorily during their registration period.

Although supervisors usually have little doubt as to their ability to undertake a supervisory role satisfactorily, this view is not always shared by the research student; there is a good case for supervisors having to undertake a proper period of apprenticeship in supervisory duties. Some shortcomings are:

- difficulties with interpersonal skills

- the level of subject specialist knowledge of the supervisors

- supervisors who have too little sense of the standard required for research degrees.

The research student may feel isolated and alarmed if time seems to pass swiftly with little sense of achievement. There are several reasons for over running the specified time for completion – approximately two years for a Master of Philosophy (M.Phil) and three years for a Doctor of Philosophy (Ph.D.) when undertaken on a full-time basis. For example:

- a slow start with failure to catch up with the schedule

- an aim for perfection

- distractions from the main programme of work

- inadequate collection of data.

To tackle a task effectively it is important that students have appropriate means at their disposal. For example, students should, if necessary, at an early stage in their programme receive formal guidance, instruction or training in research techniques. During the programme of research it is essential that there is a close and frequent contact with the supervisor (or supervisory team). Research students should be in no doubt where they stand regarding progress, achievement and likelihood of successfully completing their programme of work within an appropriate time period. If necessary the supervisor's judgement should be conveyed to the student in writing.

The following (Science and Engineering Research Council 1992) is a check list of good supervisory practice:

- Is there a departmental document available to students and supervisors, laying out the department's view on good supervisory practice?

- What steps are taken to try and make a good match between a supervisor and prospective student?

- Is the student given a reading guide before starting the programme of work?

- Does the student present a report in the first year which is assessed by people other than the supervisor?
- Does the student see the supervisor often enough?
- Are there regular occasions when the student's progress and background knowledge of the subject are both assessed?
- Is the first year assessment procedure seen as satisfactory by both student and supervisor?
- Are there occasions when the student has to make a public presentation and are these presentations satisfactory?
- How is the topic of research refined in the first year?
- When is a long term programme of research laid out and has a critical path been defined?
- Is there a point where the supervisor checks the student's record keeping to see whether it is systematic?
- Is it clear by half-way into the second year that it is possible to finish the project in the time specified?
- Does the student get a mock viva between six and twelve months before he is due to submit the thesis?

These questions apply largely to the supervisor and department in which the work is being conducted. In addition to the few which apply to the student, the following questions may be directed specifically to the student (Science and Engineering Research Council 1992):

- Have you tried to plan your work satisfactorily?
- Have you identified the major difficulties?
- Do you understand the relevant references?
- Are your records in good order and could you answer a question on something you did six months ago?
- Have you drafted the first version of any portion of the work that has been completed?
- Do other people find your written English difficult to understand?
- Are there any titles, figures or other written matter which could usefully be prepared at an early stage.

References

Collins, P.M.D. (1991) 'Quantitative Assessment of Departmental Research, Science and Engineering Policy Studies Unit of the Royal Society and the Fellowship of Engineering'. *Policy Study No. 5*, April.

Polytechnics and Colleges Funding Council (1992) *Developing Teaching: Teaching More Students, The Teaching More Students Project*. Oxonian Rewley Press.

Science and Engineering Research Council (1992) *Research Student and Supervisor: An Approach to Good Supervisory Practice*. Swindon: Science and Engineering Research Council.

de Solla Price, D.J. (1986) *Little Science, Big Science – and Beyond*. New York: Colombia University Press.

Further Reading

Bligh, D.A. (1971) *What's The Use of Lectures?* Exeter University Teaching Services.

Bligh, D.A., Jacques, D. and Warren Piper, D. (1981) *Seven Decisions When Teaching Students*. Exeter University Teaching Services.

Bruner, J.S. (1990) *Acts of Meaning*. London: Harvard University Press.

Roginson, F.P. (1961) *Effective Study*. New York: Harper and Brothers.

Chapter 5

Curriculum

...we may hope that his studies of particular subjects and combinations of subjects will bring with them habits of thought which transcend the particular content of their subject matter.

Lord Robbins

Content of the Curriculum

One of the frequent criticisms of a curriculum is that it is overloaded. Care must be exercised to ensure that the content of the curriculum can be delivered by the teaching methods proposed in the time available to students whose abilities are defined by the intake requirements.

The content of the curriculum is influenced by:

- the place of the programme of study, in a hierarchy of programmes, which allows planned progression
- a body of knowledge which gives breadth and depth
- opportunities for interdisciplinary and multidisciplinary studies.

Although many teachers contend that it is not so much what is taught but the way in which it is taught, a great deal of time and effort is spent in choosing the content of the curriculum in addition to the tuition processes which define the techniques by which the curriculum is delivered to the students.

The body of knowledge that comprises a curriculum for a programme of study is often defined by the teachers of that curriculum although professional bodies and learned societies may exert an influence on curriculum design. Knowledge can be classified into forms and fields (Hirst 1974). The former are defined by their distinctive concepts and characteristic methods of explanation, for example, mathematics and the natural sciences; the latter are defined by their subject matter (for example engineering), and draw on all forms of knowledge that can contribute to them. Consequently, it is not easy to justify the boundaries between academic knowledge and, within certain limitations, it is a good rule to define the curriculum by the strengths of the teaching team.

The hidden curriculum is often defined as the aspects of the curriculum that may be brought about, covertly, by the standards, attitudes and bias of the teachers teaching the programme. This leads to the values, organisation and methods of the teachers being transmitted to, and adopted by, the students. This may not always be beneficial. In their turn, the students may perpetuate these values and techniques.

In organising knowledge, the pertinent questions for the design of programmes of study which are comprised of largely theoretical knowledge could be (Lewis 1972)

- What are the names of the laws and theories, or their equivalents, that give structure to the knowledge covered in the programme?

- What are the postulates, theorems, and other propositions that are central to each of the theories?

- What are the headings of the classes of facts inter-related by each of the laws and theories?

- What are the references to the key works in which these laws and theories were first stated in the form taught in the course?

- What are the major limitations of each of the laws and theories?

- What are the key references that discuss and explain these limitations?

- What knowledge is presented in the programme that does not fall within the limits of applicability of the laws or theories enumerated?

- What methods have been used to organise this knowledge?

Correspondingly, for applied programmes of study (Lewis 1972):

- Upon what body or bodies of fundamental knowledge does this programme draw?

- What are the names of the laws and theories, or their equivalents, in the fundamental knowledge that give organisation to the knowledge being applied?

- What are the postulates, theorems, and other propositions that are central to each of the theories?

- Cite examples of how the laws and theories in the fundamental knowledge have been fruitfully applied.

- What practical forms of organisation in the programme take precedence over the organisation that stems from the structure of the fundamental body of knowledge?

- In what ways does the practical form of presentation increase the pedagogical efficiency as compared to a presentation based upon the structure of the fundamental body of knowledge?

- What classes of facts in the programme fall outside the limits of applicability of the laws and theories in the fundamental body or bodies of knowledge upon which the course is dependent?

Having defined the areas of knowledge, that is, the content of the curriculum, the processes by which knowledge is delivered to the students must also be defined. It is clear that many areas of knowledge may be common to many programmes of study and it is worth investigating the unifying factors which lend a measure of interdisciplinarity between programmes. Other parts of programmes which are not linked in this way may in addition be studied, which gives a multidisciplinary dimension to a programme of study.

These characteristics are often more easily introduced into programme design by the use of a modular or course unit system. Programmes are divided into discrete units, or modules, and the student may gain credits by successfully undertaking each of the modules. The final qualification, or indeed intermediate qualifications, may be achieved by the successful completion of a specified number of modules. The system provides the basis of a flexible learning programme. Provided that modules can be satisfactorily timetabled, students can negotiate programmes of study to their own specifications and undertake them at their own pace. Hence, learning programmes are tailored to individual needs and may be undertaken on a 'fast-track' basis, if required. By introducing full-time and part-time modes of study which allow changes in study modes as required, and credit accumulation and transfer, the students are not constrained by the place or time of study.

However, it is important that chosen programmes of study have appropriate breadth and depth. In addition, the integration of study units is a cause for concern. Integration can be facilitated by an appropriate choice of teaching technique, for example project work.

Sequencing

When delivering a curriculum, the order of the different parts of the curriculum need sequencing in a coherent way to achieve the learning objectives. Often, this is believed to be a hierarchical order with lower level knowledge and skills preceding the higher level of knowledge and skills. This can be done fairly easily for small parts of the curriculum but is more difficult to achieve for the entire curriculum unless it is made up of a few distinct, compartmental-ised subjects which are present throughout the whole of the course. In practice, although subjects will be fragmented, unifying aspects will be present and it is the skill of the programme designer that will ensure that the programme is delivered as a unified whole. Although the designer may judge that the curriculum is sound, with appropriate techniques to subject the student to a good quality learning experience, the learning programme may not be unified, integrated or synthesised after reception by the student.

A curriculum is designed to ensure that knowledge, skills and attitudes are transmitted to, and learned by, the student. The sequencing may be achieved in the following ways:

- a chaining sequence where later subjects build on earlier subjects
- sequencing that optimises motivation
- a problem-based sequency
- general principles leading to practical applications
- practical problems leading to the principles governing them.

As motivation correlates most closely with success, sequencing that is designed to optimise student motivation is likely to be most successful in terms of the attainment of the learning objectives of the programme of study.

Core Skills

Within the past decade there has been an attempt to incorporate, more explicitly, core skills within a curriculum. Sometimes the emphasis has been to make recommendations for vocational education (Further Education Unit 1985); more widely, it is recognised that there are aspects of personal development which play an important part in helping people to be effective and adaptable in employment. Such transferable skills are considered as personal or non-academic skills which are developed and enhanced by the processes, that is, methods of tuition, designed to deliver the curriculum. Hence, after initial instruction, these skills are integrated into the curriculum. Core skills include:

- communication and the use of language
- numeracy and an understanding and appreciation of data
- problem solving
- teamwork and interpersonal skills
- information technology
- self-appraisal skills; improving learning and performance.

It is not to be expected that all the subject matter in the curriculum is delivered using tuition methods that are designed to inculcate all core skills; nonetheless, there is much advantage to be gained in matching the tuition processes as closely as possible to core skill requirements. This can be done by placing the learning activities in a range of settings that are designed to enhance core skill development. Examples of settings that are advantageous in the development of core skills are as follows:

- seminar work
- individual project work
- team-based exercises such as project work and fieldwork
- personal research and report writing.

Core skills are statements of outcomes and, in order to assess them, performance criteria are required. These criteria are not easy to apply in practice to the learning activity and outcomes are the subject of much debate. Both teacher assessment and peer assessment are used in some cases.

National Vocational Qualifications

The National Vocational Qualification (NVQ) has been one noteworthy development (NCVQ 1991). The main aim of the award is to meet the needs of the employers. The framework of the award is designed to create a coherent classification for qualifications across five levels, that is, NVQ level 1 up to NVQ level 5. The highest level is intended to correspond to graduate level. The curriculum is presented in a modular structure and is designed to facilitate transfer and progression. Core skills are included in all qualifications to facilitate recognition of aspects of achievement that may, in the past, have been unacknowledged. Outcomes are based on skills, knowledge, understanding and ability in application. The skills, or competence, tests are, as far as possible, conducted in the workplace, although this has often been found to be unrealistic in logistical terms.

The design and structure of the NVQs on a unit basis has meant that a variety of routes to the qualification are available. This, in turn, means that the curriculum can be offered as flexible learning programmes, unlike the more rigid traditional programmes. Students can negotiate the units that they wish to achieve, the order in which they achieve them, and their pace of study. Thus, learning programmes are tailored to individual needs. The development of the NVQs has resource implications, although co-operation between colleges may reduce the overall increase in resource demands. The unit structure of the NVQs lends itself to credit accumulation and transfer systems and, in particular, the effective exploitation of the accreditation of prior experience and learning (APEL). Advantages of the NVQs are:

- they provide a flexible programme of study
- they provide a nationally recognised qualification
- prior experience and learning can be accredited
- study may be undertaken at a pace chosen by the student
- transfer and progression is facilitated
- core skills are integrated into programmes of study.

Disadvantages of NVQs are:

- the emphasis on competence skills has been at the expense of knowledge
- competences are too narrow and simplistic
- an increased level of resources is required.

However, the NVQs are at a relatively early stage of development.

Work Experience/Placement

Many programmes of study give an opportunity to students to undertake work experience. Students gain maturity and experience which affects their subsequent attitude and ability to gain from, and contribute to, their academic work when they return to college. The period of placement can vary from two weeks to one year. Students are encouraged to take as wide an interest as possible in all aspects of the activities in which they are involved. Students are often expected to enter actively into the search for suitable employment and, when placed in employment, to maintain a diary of activities. During placement, the students are visited and the visiting teacher completes a report on the quality of the experience given and the way in which the student is responding. An early visit is undertaken to ensure that the work placement is appropriate. At the conclusion of the work experience, a full report on the work done is prepared by the student. In addition, the employer is required to submit a report on, and assessment of, the student. The various reports from both employers and academic staff are retained so that the full history of the student's work placement is available. The organisation of work placements includes:

- training services handbook; placements tutor
- opportunities available; interviews and CVs; experience
- summary of anticipated conditions of service; work ethos
- main points of employment law
- general matters; safety, health and welfare
- college/employer links and liaison; tutor visits
- student requirements; log books, reports; assessment criteria.

Important factors relating to work placement are:

- What are the main aims and objectives of work experience/ placement?
- What is the relationship between college-based experience and work experience/placement?
- Is the work experience/placements scheme centrally co-ordinated in the college or organised departmentally?
- Are the placements well planned with respect to suitability, agreed aims and objectives with the employer?
- How are students and employers prepared for work placement by means of induction etc.?
- Are students visited on work placement; how often; what final record of placement is required?
- What is the learning value of the placement and what contribution does it make towards the programme and qualification?
- Are employers required to assess the student's performance on work placement; if so, what contribution does this make to the final qualification received by the student?

Design of Programmes of Study

The important considerations for curriculum design are:

- What are the aims and objectives of the curriculum?
- What is the source of the curriculum?
- What policies/procedures influence the nature of the curriculum?
- Does the individual programme of study equip students for qualification goals and/or the workplace?
- Does the curriculum include both general and specialist education; are transferable skills generated?
- Are the different elements of the curriculum appropriately integrated?
- Does the curriculum take account of individual needs?

- Are learning experiences provided which allow the practice of relevant competences?
- Are progression opportunities available?
- What arrangements are there to plan, co-ordinate and implement the programmes of study?
- Is the curriculum regularly reviewed, evaluated and updated?
- Is there sufficient resources to achieve the specified learning experiences?

Using the quality grade descriptors given in Chapter 1 the following characteristics are used to judge the quality of the curriculum in the college:

1. *Very good*, i.e., showing many of the following characteristics:
   - relevance; relates to present and future needs
   - explicit and carefully focused
   - effective use of time for individual subjects and their arrangement
   - body of knowledge that offers breadth and depth
   - state of the art and well balanced
   - cumulative knowledge and skills, which allows for planned progression
   - coherent sequencing of subjects and subject matter
   - different aspects of the curriculum allow for integrated working
   - relevant balance of all core skills
   - appropriate accreditation of the programme from professional bodies, other colleges, NVQ, etc.

2. *Good*, i.e., showing some of the good characteristics listed in (1) above with no major shortcomings

3. *Satisfactory*: i.e., sound but undistinguished, or good characteristics balanced by shortcomings:
   - satisfies students' industrial and commercial needs
   - appropriate and relevant
   - appropriate use of time constraints for most subjects

- up-to-date subject content but lacking in any aspects of the state of the art
- programme allows for adequate means of progression
- sequencing of subjects and subject content sensibly arranged
- integration achieved but sometimes in an unplanned way
- core skills being addressed but not in any structured manner
- accreditation is being achieved from professional bodies.

4. *Unsatisfactory*, i.e., showing some major shortcomings as listed in (5) below, in important areas.

5. *Poor*, i.e., showing many of the following shortcomings:
- inappropriate range of subjects having no currency value in practice
- poorly designed and confusing
- poor and unsuitable allocation of time
- subject content is dated and lacking in both breadth and depth
- progression is inhibited resulting in the need for additional programmes of study
- sequencing of information has not been considered or evaluated
- subjects and sub-subjects are delivered in a random fashion
- no attempt is made to ensure that core skills are included
- accreditation from external bodies is not considered essential.

An alternative approach for developing a grade descriptor can be made by reference to Table 5.1 in which a series of gradations facilitate the determination of the quality judgement.

Programmes of study are designed on the basis of organising the formal teaching time to provide the means by which it is assumed that learning takes place. Students use their own time for private study to reinforce and consolidate learning. However, there is presently a consideration to design courses around the

Table 5.1: Curriculum		
	Very Good: 1	*Good: 2*
Relevance	Relates to present and anticipated future needs.	Emphasises current activities of practice.
Aims and Objectives	Explicit and carefully focused.	Clear and unambiguous.
Time Constraints	Effective use of time for individual subjects and their arrangement.	Good use of time allocation and timetabling arrangements.
Content	A body of knowledge which offers breadth and depth. State of the art and well balanced.	A good body of knowledge which offers breadth and depth and is well balanced.
Progression	Cumulative knowledge and skills which allows for planned progression.	Curriculum allows for planned progression.
Sequencing	Coherent sequencing of subjects and subject matter.	Sequencing of curricula is generally appropriate.
Integration	Different aspects of the curriculum allow for integrated working.	Programmes provide for integration at all levels.
Core Skills	Relevant balance of all core skills.	Good balance of all core skills.
Accreditation	Appropriate accreditation of the programme from professional bodies, other colleges, NVQ, etc	Accreditation by professional and national bodies.

Table 5.1: Curriculum		
Satisfactory: 3	*Unsatisfactory: 4*	*Poor: 5*
Satisfies students and industrial and commercial needs.	Fails to meet the wider needs of students and workplace requirements.	Inappropriate range of subjects having no currency value in practice.
Appropriate and relevant.	Ambiguous and ill-defined.	Poorly designed and confusing.
Appropriate use of time constraints for most subjects	Distortion in emphases between competing subjects	Poor and unsuitable allocation of time.
Up to date subject content but lacking in any aspects of the state of the art.	Subject content is out of date and lacking in breadth.	Subject content is dated and lacking in both breadth and depth.
Programme allows for adequate means of progression.	Progression criteria has not been properly considered.	Progression is inhibited resulting in the need for additional programmes of study.
Sequencing of subjects and subject content is sensibly organised.	Sequencing of the curriculum is erratic disadvantaging the learning process.	Sequencing of information has not been considered or evaluated.
Integration is achieved but sometimes in an unplanned way.	There is no attempt to plan for integrating the subjects in the programme.	Subjects and sub-subjects are delivered in a random fashion.
Core skills being addressed but not in any structured manner.	Some core skills are not being properly considered.	No attempt is made to ensure that core skills are included.
Accreditation is being achieved from professional bodies.	Accreditation of programmes has still to be obtained.	Accreditation from outside bodies is not considered essential.

students' independent learning time with the formal teaching hours, somewhat reduced, to support these independent learning activities. Class contact time is being perceived as the support for more effective independent learning. This is commensurate with an emphasis on study skills.

Other features include:

- a project-based approach to studies with both understanding and competency as essential objectives

- a recognised qualification; for example certificate, diploma, degree for successfully completed parts of each programme of study

- improved accreditation of prior experience and learning procedures to facilitate acceptance with advanced standing on a programme of study

- transfer to other institutions, if necessary due to change of work place, etc., facilitated by the credit accumulation and transfer system.

Franchising

The franchising of programmes of study, or parts of programmes, by HE colleges to FE colleges has seen considerable expansion during the past few years. The reasons for this expansion include:

- the expansion of access to HE

- relief of accommodation problems in the HE colleges.

The establishment of the franchised programme of study in the FE college is best undertaken by a formal validation or accreditation process undertaken by the HE institution. In this way, the proposal can be scrutinised formally and with rigour. The validation process tends to concentrate on the written scheme and the human and physical resources available, for example, staffing, accommodation and equipment, rather than teaching strategies and standards, or the overall ambience of the college as a community.

A major concern for franchising colleges is the degree of rigour with which quality is monitored and evaluated by the FE college. In arrangements where the HE college formally monitors procedures in FE, this is beneficial to all involved. Examinations and assignments are set by the franchising college, whose staff act as moderators. Staff development is often a high priority, particularly for staff who have had relatively little experience of HE before franchising arrangements were established. The benefits of franchising may be summarised as:

- courses available locally for students for whom travel is difficult
- flexibility as regards modes of attendance
- increased opportunities to enrol in HE despite the greater student demand
- progression opportunities.

The main difficulties to be overcome are:

- development of staff in the FE colleges
- improvement of learning resources (for example libraries) to satisfy the needs of the HE students
- improvement of quality monitoring and evaluation in FE
- establishing an FE college ethos which is more compatible with an HE culture.

References

Employment Department, NCVQ (1991) *Guide to National Vocational Qualifications*, March. Employment Department.

Further Education Unit (1985) *Core Competences in Engineering*. FEU.

Hirst, P. (1974) *Knowledge and the Curriculum*. London: Routledge Kegan Paul.

Lewis, R.W. (1972) 'Course content in structured knowledge areas'. *Improving College and University Teaching*, 20, 131.

Further Reading

Cribb, M., Dixon, K. and Price, R. (1989) *Planning a Curricular Response*. Further Education Unit.

Further Education Unit (1992) *Vocational Education and Training in Europe*. FEU.

Chapter 6

Standards and Assessment

Asking an educationalist for a professional judgement is no different from asking a barrister for counsel's opinion or a medical specialist for a prognosis or an arts expert for an appraisal.

Heythrop Park Conference

Institutional Quality Control Procedures

The majority of colleges execute their quality control, assurance procedures and maintenance of standards through their academic boards or their equivalents. The procedures have the following aims:

- the holistic development of their students including their better preparation for employment
- the maintenance and enhancement of the quality of education experienced by their students
- the assurance that new programmes of study are developed to the appropriate standards and quality
- that subject development is taking place whereby programme inputs are at the appropriate level and content to reflect current developments
- to encourage all staff to be involved in review, monitoring, evaluation and validation as a part of their own personal development.

The setting of standards is usually determined by the academic boards that are also responsible for assessing whether they are actually being achieved. The control of quality is seen as a programme of study team activity on a continuous basis, to examine whether or not the specified standards and aims are being maintained and improved. It is also desirable that there is some form of external check or audit on standards, normally through an external examiner or moderator but also by accrediting organisations, such as the professional bodies, the Higher Education Quality Council (HEQC), the funding councils' inspectors and other government assessors and auditors.

Programme of Study Review Systems

Programme of study review systems provide the key framework for improving quality within a college. They are normally undertaken on a quinquennial basis. They seek to develop systems for the evaluation of quality during the different stages of a programme of study's life by assessing the adequacy of:

The programme review:

- what this involves
- the reasons for, and scope of, the review
- a clear specification of the aims and objectives of the review
- the identification of performance criteria
- the progress towards improved standards.

The reviewers:

- the staff involved, i.e., individuals or the whole team
- other staff in the college
- external assessors.

The evidence gathered:

- the sorts of information used, both numerical and descriptive
- information from students and employers
- the information from other sources, e.g. external examiners, professional bodies
- the use that is made of this information.

The review result:

- are the issues on quality addressed
- the action that follows the review
- accountability from the college
- feedback.

Programme of Study Validations

Most programmes of study come into being either because of the desire of a college, aspirations of teachers in a department, the needs of commerce and industry or the demands by prospective students. Before programmes are offered to students they are normally the subject of an internal and external validation. These provide an indication of the proposed standards that can be expected and how they will be achieved. This is done to satisfy college managers that the programme meets certain criteria and for recognition by external bodies that may offer exemptions from their own examination system to holders of the qualification. Such events help to:

- promote a corporate spirit through a wider understanding by involving teachers across other disciplines
- develop a quality culture through the spreading of good practice
- make programme teams more responsive to the needs of students and employers
- critically examine the way that programmes are delivered
- assure college managers that quality standards are being maintained.

The following criteria are used when judging the reliability of the validation event. This may take place over several days:

- expertise of the validators
- philosophy of the programme of study proposal
- aims and objectives of the programme
- capability of the programme team to deliver the proposed curriculum
- resourcing of the proposed programme
- assessment strategy capability
- amount of documentation which is required
- procedures adopted to provide a scrutiny of all relevant aspects of the programme
- means of protecting an approved programme from sectional interests.

Programme of Study Management

Programme of study management is undertaken by a team of teachers who are responsible for the actual delivery of the particular programme. The programme of study leader or director occupies the key role in the management of the process, in terms of its efficiency and effectiveness. In addition, he or she may be supported by: admissions, year, subject, placements and personal tutors. There will be a job description for each of these which identifies their roles, responsibilities and accountability. Their work is not restricted to reaction, dealing with problems when they arise, but includes developing the programme in order to improve or enhance its quality, attractiveness and reputation. The various members of the team ensure that the programme is running according to plan and that students are maintaining progress. Their work includes:

- programme and lecturer timetables
- room allocations
- registration
- co-ordination of assessments
- recruitment: students, teachers
- appointment and mentoring of part-time and associate teachers
- liaising with outside organisations, e.g. professional bodies, employers
- student handbooks
- resource needs for the programme across the college
- liaison with external examiners or moderators
- operating the programme of study committees and evaluations
- responding to central college policy initiatives.

In determining whether the programme management is effective the following need to be considered:

- frequency of programme team meetings and the recording of minutes
- job descriptions of the programme managers

- use of mentoring and induction processes for all new teachers
- monitoring of attendance and student performance
- efficiency in the design of student and teacher timetables to allow for the best use of time
- initiatives and developments that have been introduced during the past three years
- processes employed to reduce student non-completions
- procedures for covering for absent colleagues who are ill or attending courses
- current issues which are being discussed.

Programme of Study Monitoring and Evaluation

The second phase of helping to maintain and improve the standards of a programme of study is through the annual monitoring and evaluation process. In some colleges this is looked upon only as an annual event. However, a clever and committed programme team will consider this as a continuous process, striving to install quality improvements and attempting to anticipate and rectify problems before they arise. In order to demonstrate the effectiveness of college services a variety of data on student feedback and performance indicators is analysed. Programme of study monitoring and reviews are undertaken to:

- check that the aims and objectives of the programme, which are described in the study documents, are being properly implemented
- ensure that problems that have arisen are properly recorded along with their remedy and outcome of action
- establish that resources are being managed effectively and efficiently
- confirm that the principles, policies, procedures and regulations are being observed.

The formal review may be carried out at team meetings held each term and cover the items listed in Table 6.1, in addition to other routine business:

Table 6.1: Programme of study agenda

	Autumn term	Spring term	Summer term
Enrolment statistics	*		
Student evaluation	*		*
External examiners' reports	*		
Retention statistics		*	
Future programme developments		*	
Introduction of new technologies		*	
Teaching strategies		*	
Research and development		*	
Resource needs		*	
Student assessment			*
Employer questionnaires			*
Cohort statistics			*
Student destinations			*
Added value analysis			*
Action plan			*

The minutes of these meetings are recorded and then evaluated by the senior managers in the department prior to the preparation of the annual programme report for the approval of the academic board that will offer comment, advice, guidance or direction. The report records the events that have taken place and will evaluate what has or has not been achieved. The academic board, in attempting to remedy any shortcomings, will be supportive rather than inquisitional. The outcomes of the programme evaluations result in:

- more positive attitudes
- dissemination of good practices

- critical analysis
- feedback and follow up mechanisms
- clarity of purpose
- reductions in administration
- encouraging staff to take responsibility
- rationale for actions
- shift of emphasis from monitoring to evaluation
- accountability
- quality improvements.

Further criteria for judging the quality of the procedures employed are the:

- achievement in the validity in standards
- consistency across the college
- accomplishment of measured improvements in quality
- encouragment of accountability
- simplicity and lack of bureaucracy
- operation costs which are not prohibitive.

External Examiners and Moderators

The work of the external examiner and moderator is central to the maintenance of standards of a programme. It is their key role to ensure that assessment is appropriate and effective. External examiners cannot check every piece of assessed work and it is not their duty to double mark all assignments and examination papers. They will be concerned that, according to the procedures recommended by the programme committee and to which the academic board adhere a proper, appropriate and rigorous control of standards has been maintained. Their role is essentially an audit of the process. Colleges that use a proforma, to which the report is addressed, generally achieve a better consistency in the recommendations and checking of the process.

The external examiners are appointed on the recommendation of a programme of study's board to the academic board of the college. College moderators and assessors are appointed by the validating bodies. On some programmes the appointment must be done with the approval of a professional body, where the programme provides for exemption from the professional body's own examinations. In these cases the professional body also requires the report to be copied to it for its analysis and approval. Colleges have established criteria for the appointment, duties involved and responsibilities of their external examiners. External examiners will require a copy of their job description, which outlines duties and responsibilities. In order to undertake their work effectively the external examiners must be:

- judge each student impartially
- compare the students' performance with that of other comparable programmes
- approve the form and content of the proposed examination papers
- be consulted on matters which relate to the students' progression
- attend examiners' meetings
- have access to all matters relating to assessment
- have the right to moderate the marks of the internal examiners
- have the right to conduct a *viva voce* for any student
- ensure that the assessments are in accordance with the programme of study schemes
- submit a written report.

The external examiner's reports include:

- summary of duties undertaken
- extent of involvement in the assessment
- comments on
  - scripts and other assessments
  - students by cohort and individual cases
  - assessment procedures, draft papers and marking schemes
  - consistency in results
  - the workings of the examination board

- the programme of study in general
- developments and amendments
- any recommendations.

At the end of a term of office it is proper for an external examiner to include the following items in a final report:

- review of the programme of study assessments

  - examinations
  - assignments
  - contribution of work experience

- general impression on the quality of the candidates
- the level of the students' achievements.

Moderators normally prepare their reports to suit the requirements of their sponsoring body. The contents are not dissimilar to those of external examiners. The effectiveness of external examiners and moderators can be assessed as follows:

- promptness of dealing with queries, scripts, etc.
- promptness in submitting the report
- reporting, which deals with the issues identified above
- comprehensive coverage of the points outlined above.

Some colleges grade all the reports on their programmes of study received from external bodies as an indication of the service that is provided. However, colleges are often not well equipped at verifying the appointment and subsequent performance of external examiners. A recent survey (Department For Education 1992) suggested that as many as 25 per cent of external examiners were not performing their tasks effectively and failed to guide and advise departments properly; their reports sometimes contained little guidance, provided limited evaluation and failed to be effective through late submission.

Assessment

In the final analysis, the quality of learning is assessed by the colleges themselves through their examination procedures, which have been monitored by the external examiners or moderators. By studying examination question papers, the worked solutions and the candidates' examination scripts, and through looking at assignments, coursework, projects and students' note books, it is possible to form an opinion of the standard of the programme in comparison with similar programmes elsewhere. Examination patterns and strategies will, of course, be different, with some colleges placing a greater emphasis upon continuous assessment rather than end of session examinations. It is important to discover whether:

- the assessment model adequately tests the student's performance in terms of knowledge, skills, understanding and application
- the work submitted is the student's own
- it reflects a fair performance or expectation by the student
- consistency is achieved.

A greater emphasis is now being focused upon students' problem solving abilities, that is, application, rather than solely understanding or remembering the principles involved. This is reflected in the current development of the NVQs at all levels of learning (see Chapter 5). Programme assignments also reflect this philosophy by allowing students access to wider information sources, in order to avoid solely testing a student's recall ability. It is also necessary to consider how the level of the students' performance has been reflected in award classifications, and to ensure that the distribution of grades is appropriate. However, with the impact of mass higher education it may become necessary, for expediency, to pay less attention to honours classifications, and put a greater emphasis upon pass or fail programmes only. The introduction of mass higher education also places a burden upon teachers regarding assignment monitoring and it is important that programme of study schemes are capable of their effective execution. Some programme managers have considered other assessment procedures, for example the introduction of computer marked assignments and the use of student peer groups. The examination of the students' work will consider:

- level relevant to the year and type of programme
- integration to reflect working situations
- practical problems to reflect the real world

- quantity
- quality in terms of presentation and breadth and depth of solutions
- examiner commentary
- criteria and mark distribution
- consistency, fairness and thoroughness of marking.

Each programme of study provides an assessment plan that makes clear to both teachers and students:

- **Purpose**
  - diagnostic – for gaining information about the student and including APEL
  - formative – for feedback to students on their performance
  - grading – for measures of student attainment.
- **Methods** which reflect the aims and objectives of the programme. These must provide valid and reliable results. The different methods used must offer some consistency on the student's overall performance.
- **Criteria** students must be informed of the criteria that will be applied to the assessment.
- **Timing** programmes must be prepared to assist both the teachers and the students.
- **Management**
  - for monitoring and recording student performances
  - for student feedback
  - for the internal monitoring of the assessment process.
- **Regulations** that the whole process complies with the programme documentation.

Cohort Analyses

The quality of provision can also be measured in terms of the cohort progression. This is used as an indicator for minimum time completions, although it is recognised that some students need to study for a longer period of time and, for various reasons, such as the need for employment, some students will temporarily leave programmes of study prematurely. Table 6.2 provides typical non-completion and failure rates which occur in a number of programmes of study. It includes students who start and those who join at different stages. It also counts students who leave prematurely, for whatever reason, and those who fail to obtain an award within the prescribed time period.

Table 6.2: Typical non-completion rates
(Audit Commission and Ofsted 1993)

	Withdrawal %	Failure %	Cumulative %
A -Level	10–15	15–20	25–35
FE	10–20	10–25	20–45
HE	5–10	10–20	15–30

Success rates are only modest on all kinds of programmes of study. Non-completion rates are higher in further education than in higher education, largely because students are accepted onto programmes with less restrictive and prescriptive entry qualifications. Non-completions are also rising due to widening access; unsuitability of programmes; second choice in preference to employment; financial hardship, and so forth. The percentages vary across subject disciplines. Colleges are able to record accurately the reasons for students' withdrawals in most of the cases and these help with the future planning of the programme of study. Where the 'not known' factor is higher than shown in Table 6.3, this indicates a less than satisfactory monitoring system. The following represent the major reasons for withdrawal:

Table 6.3: Reasons for students leaving full-time programmes in further and higher education

	Further Education (1991)	Higher Education (1991)
To employment	20	10
Personal reasons	20	20
Changed study	18	20
Dissatisfied	4	5
Financial problems	2	15
Not known	10	15

Added Value

Just as no accountant would judge a business operation by gross sales, but rather operating profit with a proper assessment of input costs, so it is sensible to judge the academic effectiveness of a college by the added value achieved. When calculated for the individual student, added value can be determined but is elusive to interpretation as it is subject to the vagaries of many factors, some personal, suggesting that it is difficult to predict the performance of any one student with certainty. On a group basis, it is possible to achieve a better understanding of added value with the expectation that a group, well qualified on enrolment, will perform better overall than a poorly qualified group, despite wide variations in the expected individual performances of some members of both groups (Christopherson 1980).

To calculate added value the following information is necessary:

- input profile points
- output profile points
- withdrawal rates
- age profiles.

Appendix 8 demonstrates the procedures used for the calculation of added value which uses a common currency for input and output qualifications. Figure 6.1 is based on a typical group-analysis for the degree results of twelve groups (cohorts) of engineering students; the part-time students are more mature and a factor of 6 per cent (Bourner and Hamed 1987) should be used to adjust the part-time results downwards. The effect of students' withdrawals is included and, in some cases, reduces the apparent added value by almost 50 per cent. Initial conclusions are as follows:

- the added values for the full-time and part-time groups are not substantially different; as expected, the results for the part-time students show more variability

- students' withdrawals should be included for a valid estimate of added value.

Added value can be used to investigate the relative performance of different programmes of study in, and between, colleges; in addition, by analysing the performance of different groups of students, for example:

- ethnic minority students

- women students

- high ability students

- low ability students

- disadvantaged students.

In this way the strengths and weaknesses of a college can be assessed and remedial action taken if found necessary.

It is noted that, for the engineering cohorts in Figure 6.1, the subjects required for eligibility for enrolment bear a closer resemblance to the subjects studied on the programme of study than do entry qualifications for many other programmes of study. In the latter case, a less predictable relationship is often the result. A typical example is shown in Figure 6.2. Despite a relatively small variation in the input profile, the groups of students on some programmes of study achieved only half the added value of others, that is, some cohorts achieved, on average, one honours classification lower than students on a corresponding programme of study.

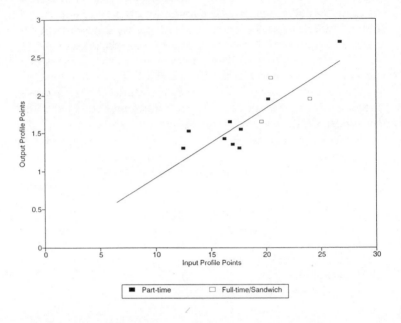

Figure 6.1: Added value for groups of engineering students

Other, more ominous issues which have been raised by added value analysis are:

- the tendency of some boards of examiners to exercise generous discretion
- the failure of some external examiners to carry out their duties effectively (Department For Education 1992).

There is scope to judge the relative effectiveness of programmes of study based on an amalgam of unit costs and added values. For example, taking added value as a measure of student satisfaction or dissatisfaction, the ratios of unit costs to added value is a valid

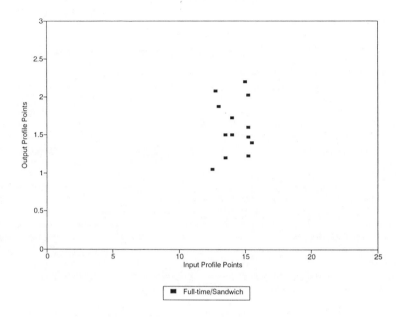

Figure 6.2: Added value for student groups

procedure by which to compare the relative effectiveness of programmes of study.

Finally, it should be noted that the added value analysis outlined measures the academic achievement of student groups. As like with like is compared, that is, academic input qualifications and academic output qualifications, it is not unusual to discover a degree of correlation. Educational research (Hudson 1967, Watley 1968) suggests that students' life performances are often not linked to academic achievement.

Using the quality grade descriptors given in Chapter 1 the following characteristics are used to judge the quality of the assessment and recording of progress in the college:

1. *Very good,* i.e., showing many of the following characteristics:
   - effective college policy on quality control
   - clear programme review systems
   - reputable validation events
   - high quality documentary evidence
   - action by college to all external reports
   - well directed programme of study
   - clever and committed programme team
   - well organised student timetables
   - appropriate number of team meetings
   - development of new initiatives
   - wide range of assessment methods with some emphasis on assessment contributing to learning
   - programme of assessments with criteria and key dates
   - emphasis upon base and application knowledge
   - fair and consistent marking
   - very few student non-completions
   - high pass rates and grades
   - high added value
   - first destinations recorded for students
   - programme monitoring of key issues
   - regular monitoring of teaching quality
   - detailed and helpful external examiners/moderators reports.

2. *Good,* i.e., showing some of the good characteristics listed in (1) above with no major shortcomings.

3. *Satisfactory*: i.e., sound but undistinguished, or good characteristics balanced by shortcomings:
   - policy for quality control
   - adequate programme review systems

- documentation meets minimum criteria
- college expects a response on comments from external reviewers
- programmes of study are adequate
- teachers work together as the programme team
- student timetables follow standard patterns
- assessment follows standard patterns
- students are provided with programmes for assessment
- emphasis relies upon formal testing
- students receive helpful guidance on their work
- non-completion rates are in line with national patterns
- national pass rate levels
- added value is still being considered
- destinations are recorded for most students
- programme monitoring provides accurate picture
- reactive monitoring of teaching quality takes place
- external examiners and moderators reports refer to assessment only.

4. *Unsatisfactory*, i.e., showing some major shortcomings as listed in (5) below, in important areas.

5. *Poor*, i.e., showing many of the following shortcomings:
- no policy for quality control
- reviews are not undertaken
- documentation relies only on standard published information
- college has no mechanisms for dealing appropriately with external reports
- programme is poorly structured
- team members do not support each other
- student timetables are inefficient and waste time
- assessment fails to test the adequacy of the students
- assessment programmes are not provided

Table 6.4: Assessment and recording of progress		
	Very Good:1	*Good:2*
Quality Control Process	Effective college policy on quality control. Clear programme review systems. Reputable validation events.	Good college quality control system. Helpful programme review systems.
	High quality documentary evidence.	Good quality documentation.
	Action by college to all external reports.	Evidence of college responses to reports.
Management	Well directed programme of study.	Clear programme direction.
	Clever and committed programme team.	Committed programme team.
	Well organised student timetables. Appropriate number of team meetings. Development of new initiatives.	Carefully planned student timetables. Awareness to new initiatives.
Assessment	Wide range of assessment methods with some emphasis on assessment contributing to learning. Programme of assessments with criteria and key dates. Emphasis upon base and application knowledge.	Good range of different assessment methods. Assessment programmes with key dates. Emphasis upon problem solving.
	Fair and consistent marking	Helpful lecturer commentary.

Table 6.4: Assessment and recording of progress		
Satisfactory:3	*Unsatisfactory:4*	*Poor:5*
Policy for quality control. Adequate programme review systems.	No overall policy for quality control. Programme review systems are of an *ad-hoc* nature.	No policy for quality control. Reviews are not undertaken.
Documentation meets minimum criteria. College expects a response on comments from external reviewers.	Documentation is lacking in many respects. College does not always follow up reports from external reviewers.	Documentation relies only on standard publications. College has no mechanisms for dealing appropriately with external reports.
Programmes of study are adequate. The teachers work together as the programme team. Student timetables follow standard patterns.	Little attention is given towards the details of the programme. The team members tend to work independently. Student timetables are poorly arranged.	The programme is poorly structured. The team members do not support each other. Student timetables are inefficient and waste time.
Assessment follows standard patterns. Students are provided with programmes for assessment. Emphasis relies upon formal testing. Students receive helpful guidance on their work.	Assessment is traditional with an emphasis upon end tests. Programmes are not co-ordinated across subjects. Assessment is largely restricted towards end of year examinations. Work is sparingly marked and returned late to students and marking is often inconsistent. Marking schemes are not used.	Assessment fails to test the adequacy of the students. Assessment programmes are not provided. Assessment tests only the students' knowledge base and the recall of information. Work is frequently not marked until the end of the year and students have little knowledge of their strengths and weaknesses.

Table 6.4: Assessment and recording of progress		
	Very Good:1	Good:2
Completions	Very few student non-completions.	Few non-completions.
	High pass rates and grades.	High pass rates.
	High added value.	Added value achieved.
	First destinations recorded for all students.	Known first destinations of most students.
Monitoring	Programme monitoring addresses key issues.	Programme monitoring identifies main issues.
	Regular monitoring of teaching quality. Detailed and helpful external examiners/ moderators reports.	Some monitoring of teaching. External examiners and moderators reports deal with main issues.

- assessment tests only the students' knowledge base and the recall of information
- work is frequently not marked until the end of the year and students have little knowledge of their strengths and weaknesses
- drop out rates are very high resulting in non-viable programmes
- pass rates are low
- added value is not considered to be useful
- destinations are not known
- monitoring is not done
- monitoring of teaching has not been considered
- reports fail to address essential issues and are too late to be of use.

An alternative approach for developing a grade descriptor can be made by reference to Table 6.4 in which a series of gradations facilitate the determination of the quality judgement.

Table 6.4: Assessment and recording of progress		
Satisfactory:3	Unsatisfactory:4	*Poor:5*
Non-completions are in line with national patterns. National pass rate levels. Added value is still being considered. Destinations are recorded for most students.	Drop out rates are much higher than the national levels. Pass rates below national levels. Added value if measured would be low. Destinations are not recorded.	Drop-out rates are very high resulting in non-viable programmes. Pass rates are low. Added value is not considered to be useful. Destinations are not known.
Programme monitoring provides an accurate picture. Reactive monitoring of teaching takes place. External examiners and moderators reports refer to assessment only.	Monitoring is poorly done. Monitoring of teaching never takes place. Reports are frequently late in their arrival and provide little information for the team.	Monitoring is not done. Monitoring of teaching has not been considered. Reports fail to address essential issues and are received too late to be of use.

References

Audit Commission and Ofsted (1993) *Unfinished Business. Full-time Educational Courses for 16–19 year olds.* London: HMSO.

Bourner, T. and Hamed, M. (1987) *Entry qualifications and degree performance, 10.* London: CNAA Development Services Publication.

Christopherson, D. G. (1980) *Are A-level Grades Good Predictors of Subsequent Success in the Profession of Engineering?* Seminar Paper, Education and Training Group, Institution of Civil Engineers.

Department for Education (1992) *Built Environment Education in the Polytechnics and Colleges.* London: Department For Education.

Hudson, L. (1967) *Contrary Imaginations.* London: Methuen/Penguin.

Watley, D.J. (1968) 'Career progress of merit scholars'. *National Merit Scholarship Corporation Research Report, Vol.4, No.1.*

Further Reading

British Standards Institution (1987) *BS 5750 Quality Systems.* London: BSI.

Employment Department (1992) *Labour Market and Skills Trends*. London: Employment Department.

Employment Department (1993) *Assessment Issues in Higher Education*. London: Department of Employment.

Further Education Unit (1989) *Towards an Educational Audit*. FEU

HMI Invitation Conference (1989) *In Pursuit of Quality: An HMI View*. *Quality in Higher Education*. Heythrop Park Proceedings, June.

PCFC/CNAA (1990) *The Measurement of Added Value in Higher Education*. London: Council for National Academic Awards.

Smithers, A. and Robinson, P. (1989) *Increasing Participation in Higher Education*. BP Educational Service.

Smithers, A. and Robinson, P. (1991) *Beyond Compulsory Schooling, A Numerical Picture*. The Council for Industry and Education.

University Management Statistics and Performance Indicators, 1990

(Source: University Management Statistics and Performance Indicators, CVCP/UFC, 1990)

Expenditure in Academic Departments (by Cost Centre)

FTE Academic Staff

E1   Expenditure per FTE student

E2   Expenditure per FTE academic staff

E3   Expenditure on support staff per FTE academic staff

E4   Expenditure on equipment per FTE academic staff

E5   Research income per FTE academic staff

Students and Staff (by Cost Centre)

FTE Student Load

E6   Research postgraduates as a % of FTE students

E7   Taught postgraduates as a % of FTE students

E8   All postgraduates as a % of FTE students

E9a Ration of FTE students to FTE teaching staff

Expenditure on central Administration

E10 Central administrative expenditure as a % of grand total expenditure

E11 Pay expenditure as a % of central administrative expenditure

E12 Central administrative expenditure per FTE student

E13 Central administrative expenditure per FTE academic staff

Expenditure on Libraries

E14 Library expenditure as a % of total general expenditure

E15 Publications expenditure as a % of library expenditure

E16 Library pay expenditure as a % of library expenditure

E17 Library expenditure per FTE student

E18 Library expenditure per FTE academic staff

E19 Expenditure on books per FTE student

E20 Expenditure on periodicals per FTE student

Expenditure on Computer Services

E21 Computer services expenditure as a % of total general expenditure

E22 Computer services pay expenditure as a % of total computer services expenditure

E23 Computer services expenditure per FTE student

E24   Computer services expenditure per FTE academic staff

Expenditure on Premises
E25   Total premises expenditure as a % of total general expenditure
E26   Premises pay expenditure as a % of premises expenditure
E27   Heat, water and electricity expenditure as a % of total general expenditure
E28   Cleaning and custodial services expenditure as a % of total general expenditure
E29   Repairs and maintenance as a % of total general expenditure
E30   Telephone expenditure as a % of total general expenditure
E31   Total premises expenditure per FTE student
E32   Premises pay expenditure per FTE student
E33   Heat, water and electricity expenditure per FTE student
E34   Cleaning and custodial services per FTE student
E35   Repairs and maintenance per FTE student
E36   Telephone expenditure per FTE student

Expenditure on Careers Services and Student Organisations
E37   Careers services expenditure per FTE student
E38   Grants to student organisations per FTE student

First Destinations of First Degree Graduates by Subject
E39   Destinations as at 31 December after graduation, UK totals by academic subject

First Destinations of First Degree Graduates by University
E40   Total graduates with known destinations
E41   Graduates with destination 'unemployment or short-term'
E42   Predicted value of indicator E41
E43   Difference between indicators E42 and E41
E44   Difference per hundred graduates

First Destinations: National Proportion of 'Unemployed or Short-term' by Subject Undergraduate Success (by Academic Subject Group)
E45   Number of successful leavers
E46   Successes as a % of those ending their studies
E47   Proportion on three and four year courses
E48   Terms of attendance per success
E49   E48 relative to expected value

Qualifications of Full-time Undergraduate Entrants, 1987 to 1989 (by Academic Subject Group)
E50   Entrants with 3 or more A levels, numbers
E51   Entrants with 3 or more A levels, score
E52   Entrants with 5 or more Scottish Highers, numbers
E53   Entrants with 5 or more Scottish Highers, score

Polytechnic and Colleges Funding Council's (PCFC) Performance Indicators

(a) Scale and effectiveness indicators:
Student population
Course completion
Student achievement
Value added
Employment and client satisfaction profiles
HMI and BTEC quality profiles

(b) Level of resourcing indicators:
Index of revenue resource
Index of capital resource (equipment)
Index of capital resource (buildings)

(c) Efficiency indicators:
Index of output cost
Ratio of students to staff

(d) Source of funds indicators:
Ratio of public to total income
Ratio of private to public funds

Appendix 3

Correlation Analysis for Factors Involved in Higher Education

A first stage analysis using the key factors involved in education and training has been undertaken. It is based on several simplifying assumptions to facilitate analysis.

(i) Each grade descriptor which judges the quality of the activity/facility is valid; this is the numerical assessment 1 to 5 which corresponds to very good to poor, respectively.

(ii) Each grade descriptor is of equal validity; weightings can be used for dated information, if required.

(iii) Different sets of data are rated and ranked using a linear relationship between consolidated data; a power law can be used, if required, which will have the beneficial effect of clarifying the rankings.

(iv) When rankings coincide, averages are used for calculating the differences in rank between key factors.

The following sample coefficients of correlation were calculated:

	Staff	Accomm.	Equip.	Teaching & Learning (T/L)	Research & Consultancy	External Liaison	Overall (O/A)
T/L	0.68	0.87	0.80	1.00	0.08	0.03	0.77
Res & Con.				0.08	1.00		
O/A	0.93			0.77		0.56	1.00

Some first stage conclusions are as follows:

(i) The accommodation and equipment correlate fairly well with teaching/learning, as does the staff.

(ii) The staff correlates well with the overall assessment.

(iii) Research and consultancy correlate poorly with teaching and learning.

Appendix 4

Capital Equipment Model

A capital equipment model for a construction department with 300 FTE students and offering a typical range of first degree, technician and professional courses (drawing on a report by the Department of Education and Science 1990).

Laboratory	Cost (£,000)	Replacement cycle (years)		Annual replacement cost (£,000)	
		maximum	optimum	maximum	optimum
Heavy structures	250	15	10	17	25
Light structures	50	15	10	3	5
Geotechnics	100	15	10	7	10
Hydraulics	100	10	7	10	14
Land surveying	100	12	8	8	13
Materials	150	15	10	10	15
Highways	25	10	5	3	5
Public health	30	10	5	3	6
Environmental science	150	10	8	15	19
Information technology	175	6	4	29	44
Workshops	50	15	15	3	3
	1180			**108**	**159**

The above annual replacement estimates are based on:

- the optimum working life of the equipment which is defined as that period of time over which an item of equipment can be maintained economically and remains appropriate;

- the maximum working life of the equipment which is defined as that period of time beyond which an item of equipment becomes inappropriate or uneconomic to maintain.

For a department with 300 FTE students, the total capital outlay is over £1 million and the annual replacement costs based on the optimum and maximum working lives, respectively, are £159,000 and £108,000. As non-capital equipment is of comparable expense, it is evident that maintaining appropriate equipment indicates annual costs of the order of £1000 per FTE student. The relative costs of equipment shown in the above table are for general guidance only. The individual amounts of specialist equipment in different departments differ, often reflecting, in part, the interests and specialisms of the staff who influence academic development.

Reference

Department of Education and Science (1990) *Higher Education in the Polytechnics and Colleges: Construction.* London: HMSO.

Input From Students

An extremely important indicator of the performance of a college is the opinion of its students. Students are informed and sophisticated in their judgements of quality relating to a wide range of programme team activities from programme management to assessment procedures; in particular, the students' assessment of teaching is often perceptive.

In order to gain a balanced view of the students' perceptions about their programmes of study, guidance from the following prompts are helpful:

(i) Why did you choose your particular specialist area of study?

(ii) Why did you choose to study at this college?

(iii) Processing of applications:

- Was your application processed satisfactorily?
- Did you participate in an open day; was it well organised?
- How appropriate were the selection and induction procedures?

(iv) Programme of study organisation:

- Were your entry qualifications appropriate for your programme of study?
- Are the range and balance of the subjects in your programme of study appropriate?
- Are the timetable arrangements satisfactory?
- Have you been given a programme of study handbook; is it well designed and informative?
- Is the balance between taught and student-centred activities satisfactory?
- Is the coursework well planned?
- What are the strengths and weaknesses of your programme of study?
- What do you enjoy most about your programme?

(v) Support arrangements for study and social activities:

- Do you know the name of your personal tutor?
- Can you gain regular access to your personal tutor?
- Does the tutorial system work satisfactorily?
- Are your study skills receiving development?

- Is your programme of study delivered using techniques designed to promote learning?
- Are you receiving appropriate academic counselling? From whom?
- Have you experienced difficulties with your studies? How have these difficulties been resolved?
- Are there appropriate learning resources available to you, e.g. computers, libraries, laboratory equipment?
- Has your period of industrial placement been appropriately organised?

(vi) Progress achieved:

- Are you properly informed of what is required for you to achieve success on your programme of study?
- If you have concerns, where and how are these made known to the programme team?
- Is your coursework regularly marked and are you given guidance in areas where your performance indicates weakness?
- Are your requests for help dealt with promptly?

(vii) Outcomes:

- What is the most important outcome for you from your programme of study?
- What skills, competences, or achievements have given you a sense of confidence for your future career?
- Are you enjoying your programme of study?
- Would you recommend your programme of study to a close friend or relative?
- Would you recommend a programme of study at this college to a close friend or relative?

Evaluation of a quality grade descriptor using an intelligent knowledge based system

An intelligent knowledge based system (IKBS), using the LEONARDO shell, for obtaining the quality grade descriptor for teaching and learning is described. To facilitate understanding all objects and values are written out fully in this Appendix; the original IKBS is comprised of a shorthand version.

The knowledge base is set up by listing the rules involving the good characteristics for each activity and facility, as given in the Chapters, in order of priority. The early listings can often be designated as 'essential', the middle order as 'required', and the remainder as 'desirable'. For example, for teaching and learning, 'factual accuracy' is considered to be 'essential', 'challenge' is considered 'required' and 'schemes of work' are considered 'desirable'. The resulting amalgam of characteristics specifies the quality of the activity or facility. The advantage of using the LEONARDO shell is, as with other intelligent systems, that characteristics can be easily added to the rules of the knowledge base without interfering with the structure or arrangement of the original listings.

The following sector of the IKBS does not give all the characteristics used but a sample of typical characteristics. Others can be added, as required, by reference to the Chapters. The sector described deals primarily with the amalgam of characteristics leading to the quality grade descriptor for teaching being 'very good'. Alternative arrangements of characteristics lead to quality grade descriptors for teaching as 'good', 'satisfactory', 'unsatisfactory' or 'poor'. Completion of the rules and the corresponding 'ask' instructions result in a workable IKBS. The same process is used for the quality grade descriptors for other activities and faciities. Also for a college as a whole, if required.

1:   seek teaching

2:

3:   if information_1 is factually_accurate then a1=1

4:

5:   if information_1 is factually_inaccurate then a1=1

6:

19:   if explanation is good then a7=1

20:

21:   if explanation is satisfactory then a7=0

22:

23:   if explanation is unsatisfactory then a7=1

113: if scheme_of_ work is unsatisfactory then a20=1

114:

115: if a1=1

116: and a2=1

117: and a3=1

118: and a4=1

119: and value_1>=10

120: and a5<>-1

135: and a2<>-1

136: then teaching is very_ good

137:

138: if sum_1 is needed then value_1=a5+_ _ _+a14+

139: a15+_ _ _ _ _+a20

141:

143: ask information_1

171: ask scheme_of_work

When the IKBS is executed the operator is interrogated by the system as to the values, ie factually_accurate, satisfactory, etc., for each of the characteristics present in an activity or facility. At the end of the interrogation the system makes, by means of its inferencing capability,its judgement which is the quality grade descriptor. A further refinement being undertaken is designed to provide advice as to the means by which the quality grade descriptor of the activity or facility could be improved.

Some Performance Indicators of Research Activity

Publications: academic journals, popular journals, books, reports, edited works, proceedings.

Other outputs (Collins 1991): patents: licences: unpublished commercial and other confidential material, e.g. contract research reports: consultancies: Government and legal reports: videos: computer software: new equipment: designs: technology transfer activities: professional training.

Citations.

Esteem indicators (Collins 1991): involvement in international organisations; appointments as co-ordinators for international research studies; active involvement in national organisations such as advisory committees, boards of management, working groups, learned societies, Government bodies; participation in peer review and commissioning and funding of research; refereeing for funding agencies, journals or publishers; external assessing for academic promotion; external examining; consultancies and other links with industry; measures of satisfaction that senior customers felt about the work that they commissioned from individuals and groups; success in securing research grants and other external research income; numbers of research students; editorship of book series; reviewing for the quality media; invited papers and chairmanship of panels at national and international conferences; invitations to give distinguished lectures and to be a visiting professor in the UK and abroad; award of honorary degrees.

Research grants.

Research income per member of staff.

Grant value per paper.

Number of post-doctoral staff employed on competitive external grants.

Number of competitive research studentships held by the department.

Consultancy.

Achieving higher degrees.

Completion rates of research students.

Depending upon the level of research activity, a points grading can be allocated for each of the individual activities, for example:

- refereed publications (10 points)

- publication in a popular journal (5 points).

By this means a research profile for a research group or department can be established. The points gradation can allow for the first and higher stages of research activity being included in the overall profile. These may include:

- the formation of a research group with set targets (1 point)

- the appointment of a research student (2 points).

Clearly, the lists of activities can be long and the points designations for each activity may cause much debate, nonetheless, the proposed technique provides a measure of overall research activity but not necessarily quality. Importantly, it permits comparisons of research effort between groups and indicates changes in activity over a period of time.

Quality is reflected in:

- the level of originality of the research and investigation

- the depth of new knowledge achieved or usefulness of the artefacts.

These are not easy to judge; the following characteristics are worthy of investigation.

- does research seek its greater understanding by fragmenting or integrating knowledge?

- bodies of fundermental knowledge that underpin work

- research techniques or enabling procedures used

- intuitive, deductive or inductive processes used

- bodies of knowledge displaced or updated

- methods used to organise or evaluate the knowledge

- funding generated; value of research based on discounted cash flow or cost benefit analysis

- who or what have the research outcomes benefitted?

For applied research, the following insights are helpful (Midwinter 1993):

- is the research linked to a real problem?

- does it produce a cost-effective solution?

- can the solution be applied or, in the case of an artefact, is it manufacturable?

- does it produce a market competitive solution?

It should not be forgotten that many research programes produce trained research workers which is key performance indicator; this may often be better return on investment than the actual research work.

Reference

Collins, P.M.D. (1991) 'Quantitative Assessment of Departmental Research, Science and Engineering Policy Studies Unit of The Royal Society and The Fellowship of Engineering'. *Policy Study No. 5*. April.

Midwinter, J.E. (1993) A measure of excellence – research assessment in universities. *Institution of Electrical Engineers Review, March.*

Procedures Used for the Calculations of Input Profile, Output Profile and Added Value

Input profile: The following points are allocated to input qualifications*.

For each GCSE pass (grades A, B or C) (see note 1)	1 point
If GCSE passes include one or more English subjects	extra 1 point
If GCSE passes include one or more modern or classical foreign languages	extra 1 point
For each GCE pass at A level: (see note 1)	
Grade A	5 points
Grade B	4 points
Grade C	3 points
Grade D	2 points
Grade E	1 point

For passes in mathematics and in each of the best three of other subjects in suitable NC/ND final examinations: (see note 2)

marks less than or equal to 64%	nil
marks 65–74%	1 point
marks 75–84%	2 points
marks more than 85%	3 points

For meritorious performance in a BTEC Higher Diploma, HND or similar course providing entry to the first or second year of a degree course additional points, as assessed on merit (see note 3):

maximum 5 points

Passes in each BTEC unit at levels III or IV (no subject to be counted at both levels) up to a maximum of six subjects

assessed mark 70–79%	1 point
assessed mark 80% or above	2 points

---

* Based on the Chilver points system approved by the Joint Board of Moderators acting on behalf of the Institution of Civil Engineers and the Institution of Structural Engineers.

Other academic achievements, including qualifications for other professions additional points as assessed on merit (see note 4)

maximum 10 points

Output profile: The following points are allocated to output qualifications:

First class honours degree	4
Upper second class honours degree	3
Lower second class honours degree	2
Third class honours degree/pass/unclassified	1

Intermediate qualifications such as an HND are assessed on merit.

Added value: Defined as the ratio of the average of the output profile points divided by the average of the input profile points calculated for each group or cohort of students. Both calculations are based on the number of students initially enrolled on the cohort.

Notes

1. No subject will earn points at both GCSE level and A level.

2. Holders of BTEC (or National) Certificates or Diplomas may count points for all GCSE levels by addition to points for Certificate or Diploma examinations.

3. The words 'or similar' could include exceptional BTEC Higher Certificate or HNC results where for instance, these are taken into account as providing entry qualifications for degree courses. A pass with distinction will score 5 points, one with merit 4 points and a bare pass 3 points.

4. Credit may be given for part qualifications provided that any such part is independently classifiable.

Abbreviation and Acronyms

A	Area per FTE student
ACS	Average Class Size
A-levels	Advanced Levels
ALH	Average Lecturer Hours
ALIS	Advanced Level Information Service
APEL	Accreditation of Prior Experience and Learning
AS	Academic Staff/Support Staff Ratio
ASH	Average Student Hours
AV	Added Value
AVA	Audio Visual Aids
BS	British Standards
BTE	Buildings Expenditure/Total Expenditure
BTEC	Business and Technology Education Council
CATS	Credit Accumulation and Transfer Schemes
CNAA	Council for National Academic Awards
COTE	Consumables Expenditure/Total Expenditure
CTE	Capital Expenditure/Total Expenditure
CV	Curriculum Vitae
CVCP	Committee of Vice Chancellors and Principals
DES	Department of Education and Science
DFE	Department For Education
ECCTIS	Educational and Credit Transfer Information Service
EPOC	Employers' Perception of Course
ER	Employment Record
ExR	Examination Results
FE	Further Education
FEU	Further Education Unit
FTE	Full Time Equivalent
GCSE	General Certificate of Secondary Education
GNVQ	General National Vocational Qualification
HE	Higher Education
HEQC	Higher Education Quality Council
HMI	Her Majesty's Inspectorate
HNC	Higher National Certificate
HND	Higher National Diploma
IKBS	Intelligent Knowledge Based System
IT	Information Technology
ITE	Income/Total Expenditure
MPhil	Master of Philosophy
MTE	Mobility Expenditure/Total Expenditure
NCVQ	National Council for Vocational Qualifications
NVQ	National Vocational Qualification
OHP	Overhead Projector

PCFC	Polytechnics and Colleges Funding Council
PF	Part-time Staff Hours/Full-time Staff Hours
PFHE	Progression to FHE/Postgraduate Studies
PhD	Doctor of Philosophy
PRP	Performance Related Pay
QTL	Quality of Teaching and Learning
RO	Research Output
RoA	Records of Achievement
SDTE	Staff Development Budget/Total Expenditure
SO	Staying On Ratio
SPOC	Students' Perception of Course
SQM	Strategic Quality Management
SQ3R	Survey, Question, Read, Recall, Review
SSR	Student/Staff Ratio
STE	Staffing Budget/Total Expenditure
SU	Space Utilisation
TQM	Total Quality Management
UC	Unit Costs
UFC	Universities Funding Council
z	Properties of Catchment Areas: z-score
%A	Percentage Attendance

Index